OBJE

A book series about the hidden lives of ordinary things.

Series Editors:

Ian Bogost and Christopher Schaberg

Advisory Board:

Sara Ahmed, Jane Bennett, Johanna Drucker, Raiford Guins, Graham Harman, renée hoogland, Pam Houston, Eileen Joy, Douglas Kahn, Daniel Miller, Esther Milne, Timothy Morton, Nigel Thrift, Kathleen Stewart, Rob Walker, Michele White.

In association with

BOOKS IN THE SERIES

Drone by Adam Rothstein

Remote Control by Caetlin Benson-Allott

Golf Ball by Harry Brown

Hotel by Joanna Walsh (forthcoming)

Refrigerator by Jonathan Rees (forthcoming)

Shipping Container by Craig Martin (forthcoming)

Silence by John Biguenet (forthcoming)

Phone Booth by Ariana Kelly (forthcoming)

Glass by John Garrison (forthcoming)

Waste by Brian Thill (forthcoming)

Tree by Matthew Battles (forthcoming)

Hair by Scott Lowe (forthcoming)

Dust by Michael Marder (forthcoming)

Doorknob by Thomas Mical (forthcoming)

Blanket by Kara Thompson (forthcoming)

driver's license

MEREDITH CASTILE

Bloomsbury Academic
An imprint of Bloomsbury Publishing Inc

B L O O M S B U R Y
NEW YORK · LONDON · NEW DELHI · SYDNEY

Bloomsbury Academic
An imprint of Bloomsbury Publishing Inc

1385 Broadway
New York
NY 10018
USA

50 Bedford Square
London
WC1B 3DP
UK

www.bloomsbury.com

**BLOOMSBURY and the Diana logo are trademarks
of Bloomsbury Publishing Plc**

First published 2015

© Meredith Castile, 2015

Library of Congress Cataloging-in-Publication Data
Castile, Meredith.
Driver's license/Meredith Castile.
pages cm. – (Object lessons)
Includes index.
Summary: "A lively exploration of how the driver's license encapsulates the
contradictory values of contemporary culture and identity, and especially
freedom and security, mobility and restriction"– Provided by publisher.
ISBN 978-1-62892-913-3 (paperback) – ISBN 978-1-62892-978-2
(ePub) – ISBN 978-1-62892-564-7 (ePDF) 1. Drivers' licenses–United States.
2. Identification cards–United States. 3. Liberty–United States.
4. National security–United States. I. Title.
HE5623.C333 2015
929.9–dc23
2014029807

ISBN: PB: 978-1-6289-2913-3
ePDF: 978-1-6289-2564-7
ePub: 978-1-6289-2978-2

Series: Object Lessons

Typeset by Deanta Global Publishing Services, Chennai, India
Printed and bound in the United States of America

CONTENTS

1 America 1

2 Fake 7

3 Design 41

4 Teen 67

5 Identity 83

6 Civics 113

Notes 133
Acknowledgments 141
Index 143

1 AMERICA

Do we contradict ourselves?/Very well, then we contradict ourselves.

In the America of the ubiquitous road less traveled, the paved paradise where the bearded Bard sings the hymn of the open road and life is a restless punching through the radio and also a highway and we're going to ride it west against the night and off into the sunset, in this mythic America, we fly along in the fast lane, placing bets against flashing lights in the rearview mirror, against the dreaded sidle into the gravel and the voice at the window demanding our license. This enforcer of safe limits, the license! But also—the license, talismanic pass to life: we may flash it to fly, skydive, gamble, tattoo ourselves, pierce ourselves, marry each other, register an assault weapon, drink, smoke, chew, dance, see a striptease, see jazz in the clubs where it belongs, rent a car, travel on Amtrak, buy dildos, swords, firecrackers, spray paint ..., donate blood, file government forms with new employers, receive unemployment, be issued a birth certificate for our own newborn, adopt dogs from shelters, surrender dogs to shelters, attend sex conventions, open bank accounts, charge major purchases, vote, get senior discounts, register as a visitor at a hospital's front desk, and so on, and so on, and so on. The license is our pass, our validation, our bureaucratic identity. Presenting it is the handshake of officialdom: This is who I am, the official me. But it can also be a motion of intimacy: I'll show you mine if you show me yours. This photo is the worst photo ever taken of me—it doesn't even look like me. Will you still sleep with me now that you've seen it?

Few other objects are so pervasive, part of so many different registers of American life, as the driver's license. Embedded in our procedures and processes, open to contradictory meanings and uses, the license reveals America, the insatiable nation, wanting it all. State authority and personal expression. Freedom and security. Miles of unbroken road, unbeatable TSA checkpoints. Self-regulation, social legislation. Drunken excess, Puritan prudence. Rooting for outlaws, guarding the rule of law. Sweet sixteen, pay your own way. Government safeguards, bureaucratic fraud. City, suburb. Image, authenticity. Inclusivity, borders. National standardization, state prerogatives. The franchise as a right, the franchise as conditional. Privacy, centralized information. And more. A map, the great ideological fault lines of America, emerges as I follow the license on its course across the rugged, stubborn, oversized land that calls itself *united*.

A note on terms: during a long childhood of wide-flung travel, when I wasn't being coached to say I was from Canada

(I'm not), my parents emphasized the fact that we were from the *United States*, not *America*. "Bolivians and Mexicans and Canadians are just as 'American' as we," my father instructed. Now, in my adopted home of Vienna, my nationality is satisfyingly specific and inoffensive—*US-Amerikanerin*. Yet for this book I choose to speak mostly of America, because the symbolic life of a driver's license lives in a web of values and ideologies not coterminous with the concrete nation-state the United States. But, of course, the fantasy Americas fold over into the real one. Imagination and interpretation shape lived political realities. So alongside the laws, facts and figures of the United States, "America" figures in this book as *mythos*, a symbolic territory, a construction. The sea-to-sea vastness of the nation, a vastness webbed by interstates totaling triple our planet's circumference, facilitates such mythologizing. Andy Warhol explains:

> Everybody has their own America, and then they have pieces of a fantasy America that they think is out there but they can't see. … [Y]ou live in your dream America that you've custom-made from art and schmaltz and emotions just as much as you live in your real one.[1]

The wider the vision, the more intimately it reflects back on the seer. So too with this book. My exploration into a nation's relation to identity, transit, and personal freedom—by virtue of its breadth—cannot *not* be projective and personal. So be it. My analysis spins along grooves of an American-made mind, sounding that simultaneously banal and illuminating *thing*, the license, for the irrepressible values and contradictions with which we both, the license and I, betray our homeland.

Desperado Pilgrims

"Where are you from?" an old German on a train once asked my husband. "Kansas City." "Ah, Kansas! Bang-bang stick-'em up!" the German said. My husband got a laugh out of this, but in some ways, American culture is still defined by a kind of Wild West, renegade individualism. We are rule-breakers. We jaywalk. We value dissent. We invent. We have gut feelings. We follow gut feelings. Untrained, we are dangerous rogues. I don't believe in climate change, I don't believe in vaccination, I just don't believe in Government. Deference to scientific consensus or fact-based rationality has largely evaporated from political debate. Culturally, there is no one generally accepted way to do things, from childrearing to eating. In our heterogeneous nation, we have no one national cuisine across class barriers, and more broadly, no generally shared sense of taste. There's a reason why Anglo-Americans lack native phrases to describe the art of following an established cultural procedure. "Rugged individualism," as American culture has so often been characterized, resists the *comme il faut* or *savoir faire*. We figure it out ourselves.

But here's one representative counterexample to the lone-ranger picture of American society: our drinking laws.

No other nation has a higher minimum drinking age than the United States. While French teenagers linger along the Pont des Arts with bottles in hand, American 20-year-olds are trying to fake their way into the neighborhood bar with bogus driver's licenses ordered online from China. Youth drinking in the United States—both its legal repression and its culture of binges—is a reminder of the polarity of the national consciousness. In addition to being a nation of outlaws, inventors, free-thinkers, and deregulated capitalists, we are ever still a nation of Pilgrims with our Witch Trials, Prohibition, McCarthyism, mass imprisonment for nonviolent drug crimes, neoconservative military interventions, and so on. We may be binge-drinking desperados, but we're also law-giving Puritans. The negotiation between *laissez-faire* individualism and frameworks of social regulation: this is *the* ground-zero fault line of American political life. The recent history of the driver's license bears witness to this fact.

Pop quiz: *Which American political party corresponds with social regulation?*

In terms of the driver's license, you probably guessed wrong.

Here follows the story of how two Republican administrations—those of Ronald Reagan and George W. Bush—transformed the license from a low-profile document for administrative matters into a security document charged with preserving the safety of our citizens. In the security features of today's driver's license, the legacies of Reagan's intensified War on Drugs and Bush's War on Terror intersect. In the past thirty years, with less resistance than one would imagine from the Lone-Ranger Nation, the license has become both the primary check on youth drinking and an ever more prevalent photographic identity verifier in an era obsessed with the magical thinking that matching name and picture to a face can reveal a stranger as friend or foe.

Fear motivates. Safe passage as we range our vast country, on a highway free from teen drunks, on a flight free from terrorists: that was what we couldn't have without a safer license. And so we got a safer license.

And all the kids got fakes.

2 FAKE

Drunk

"The fact that somebody can come in and willy-nilly pick a group of people and deprive them of their privileges is beyond anything," said Wyoming politician Hardy Tate, quoted in the *New York Times*. "After a while, you just get tired of somebody else telling you what to do."[1]

The year was 1987. Six states—Wyoming, Colorado, Idaho, Montana, South Dakota, and Ohio—were allied in a standoff with the federal government. These rebels saw themselves as defending states' rights to self-determination. The federal government was trying to coerce them into raising their minimum drinking ages to 21, and they weren't having it.

"People still want to have some independence and to be able to control their own destiny," explained a South Dakota attorney general. He was then mounting his state's suit against the federal government. Argued before the Supreme Court, the plaintiffs sought to overturn the law that had triggered all the outrage: the National Minimum Drinking Age Act of 1984.

The Act mandated that 10 percent of federal highway funding would be withheld from any state with a minimum drinking age under 21. When the bill first came up, even Reagan privately questioned its reach. He'd argued over and again for state autonomy: didn't this bill go against his political values? But MADD, Mothers Against Drunk Driving, raised a fearsome clamor, and Reagan swallowed his doubts and pushed the bill: "We have no misgiving about this judicious use of Federal power." The sanctions were not so harsh as to be judged unconstitutional (Reagan hoped), but harsh enough that no state would hold out against them.

Three years later, the five Western cowboy states (and Ohio) were still resisting. "This isn't a drinking issue," said another Wyoming politician. "It is a rights issue."

But by 1988, the standoff was over. South Dakota lost in the Supreme Court. The states needed their full highway money. The rebels raised the drinking age.

The above history cannot be understood without the driver's license. Nor can the license be understood without the drinking-age crisis. For one thing, the new law came to transform the fake driver's license into a youthful institution. But first, and even more fundamentally, it completed the license's transformation into a policing tool, a *photographic identification document*. The National Minimum Drinking Age Act, a landmark reduction of states' autonomy, was the legislative event that finally forced all fifty states to issue drivers' photographs on their licenses. After all, a minimum drinking age is unenforceable without photo IDs. In a state without photo licenses, all an underage kid had to do to circumvent the law would be borrow an of-age, non-photo license. Two foot-dragging states, New York and Tennessee, refused to add mandatory photographs for noncommercial drivers to their licenses until 1986. Covert resisters, they were the last states in the union to go photographic.

And with that concession, America entered the security age.

For those of us born during or after the Reagan years, the driver's license has always been a policing instrument. A photo ID—*the* photo ID—it exists to prove who we are and that we are old enough to do what we were not allowed to do before we turned 18 or 21 or 65. Its status as a "privilege, not right" has been increasingly used as leverage to get citizens to do everything from paying library fines to cooperating in mass surveillance. In some states, if you drop out of high school, you cannot be granted a driver's license until you get a GED, reenroll, or turn 18. It seems that the timeless function of the license now is social control, not driving. But before the last decades of the twentieth century, and certainly before the so-called age of terror, the American driver's license was a simpler, humbler document.

In the post-war America of my parents' youth, a license was little more than an automotive-related document that could help validate the driver's name: cardstock, peeling lamination, no photo for many states. When my mother was born in 1946, Wyoming was a year away from instituting any sort of driver's license law; they simply didn't exist there. When American planes dropped atomic bombs on Hiroshima and Nagasaki, over a dozen states had not yet instituted behind-the-wheel driving tests.[2] History would witness the first commercially available seatbelts, Sputnik rocketing into space, Elvis Presley joining the army, and the invention of the computer modem, before the last state—South Dakota—got around to testing its drivers in 1959. (On the other hand, South Dakota was well ahead of the country of Belgium, which didn't get around to testing drivers until 1977—Which either proves that Belgians are brave souls or that testing driver aptitude is less essential than one might think.) Once upon a time, driver's licenses just weren't that big of a deal.

In the past three decades, though, the license has risen in prominence. It is now more often forged, more doggedly policed, and for the first time ever a significant national security concern. Imbued with anxiety, invested with authority and power, it is increasingly a site of political and legal struggle. What domain ultimately controls the license—the federal government or the state? Do national security concerns—drunk driving, terrorism—warrant federal intervention in state-by-state licensing? How can a license be used as a check for national security when counterfeits circulate in a global market, often outside of US extradition agreements? The American driver's license—nationally recognized, state made, globally faked: in short, a jurisdictional disaster.

Handmade

I show my hand from the start: my sympathies lie with the adolescent fakers. No doubt this stems in part from the congenital American tendency to root for the outlaw defenders of Liberty. Mixed in is nostalgia for my youthful larking about with an expired, hole-punched license from a sororal acquaintance who would later go on to architectural fame. I remember the thrill of pulling the ID out just right, so my thumb covered the give-away hole. I remember the solidarity that came from running a "pass back" operation—sending out an ID to be used a second time by an acquaintance with similar looks and no ID. And I remember my gratitude for the servers in my little urban neighborhood who saw something in me that looked old enough, or cracked enough, to warrant letting me slip in for a touch of cold comfort.

Faking it used to be a simple affair. In my father's Texas of the early 1960s, you could simply peel back the license lamination and doctor your birth year with some Wite-Out™ and a ballpoint pen. Or simpler still, you could find a sympathetic store clerk who didn't mind selling a little beer to some nice-looking 15-year-old (white) boys.

In the late 1980s—thanks to the aforementioned spotlight on underage drinking and license security—creating a fake had become a bit more elaborate. In retrospect, however, they seem like the halcyon years of alcoholically wasted youth.

I asked my husband, who grew up in a quietly affluent suburb of Kansas City in the 1980s and 1990s, to tell me his story of the era of homemade fakes.

So there we were, the six of us, sixteen years old, trying to figure out how to make an ID. This was 1990, long before any digitalization. There was some lamination going on, but not yet rows of state seals in the laminate itself. We didn't have to worry about that.

We figured out that a license, in Kansas anyway, had a kind of Polaroid look. So we decided to make an enormous license and take a Polaroid of it. … We got a gigantic piece of paper from those giant rolls they have in school art classrooms and spent a couple hours drawing the license to scale. It was pretty good. The artist among us went on to art school later.

Then we just had my friend Craig stand in front of a blue square on the giant license, took a Polaroid of the whole thing, cropped it and laminated it.

[ME: *I don't understand. Couldn't you see Craig's torso?*]

Luckily, the photo was on the bottom left of the Kansas license. And there was no boundary around the photo— just a background. So it worked. … Back then, the Kansas DMV had a color-coding system curtain that served as the head-shot background. Dark blue, I think it was, meant "of age." So we used some dark blue paper from the art room for the "photo" background.

[*What was the identity you guys chose?*]

Jeff Mase (pronounced "Mace"), aged 22. We thought that name was a hilarious average-white-guy name.

[*And was the fake convincing?*]

Well, it worked. The only major flaw was the back of the license. The real ones had some complicated graphics that had to do with organ donation. So the fake didn't have a backside, really. If a store clerk flipped it over, the jig was up.

[*What happened when you got found out?*]

Actually, there were clerks who looked at the back, thought a moment, and then still sold us alcohol. We had good luck in the places with immigrant employees or in the shabbier-looking stores that were out of the way that didn't seem to do much business.

[*How many times did you use the ID?*]

Oh, all the time. Four times a week. Maybe five. All through high school. And we also used it to rent hotel rooms for parties—you had to be over 18 to rent a hotel room. One time the police nearly caught us, but we escaped out the window just in time.

[*So "Jeff Mase" got away?*]

Well, the hotel had a bad photocopy of the ID, and the police sent it around to the local high schools, just in case it matched a student. Our school office reported back that it looked like Craig, and the police questioned him, but he kept cool, and the image quality was too bad to prove anything.

Later I ask my (now admirably responsible) husband how he thinks his youth might have been different had the license been too difficult to fake. Would he have been more on track, less the diamond-in-the-rough honor student gone awry? "Nah," he said. "I'd probably have drunk less—and done more drugs."

Digital

I came of age only a decade after my husband's antics. But when I flew eastward to start college—on September 18, 2001—the climate around IDs had shifted dramatically. It had shifted over mere minutes with the collective national trauma of the falling towers, and it shifted over years with digitization. By 2001, making a fake without a computer was unthinkable. You'd hear of an acquaintance's acquaintance who had ID-making equipment (the right printer, laminator, etc.) and charged $150 a pop; the rate can be higher these days, up to $300 for the highest quality counterfeits. Admittedly, you can make terrible homemade fakes without much work by scanning an existing license, altering the photo and text in Photoshop, printing, and laminating. But they're of such limited use it's probably not worth the trouble.

The popular website wikiHow explains a "professional method" that goes far beyond the scan-and-alter slapdash fake. Requiring both technical and technological skill, the successfully executed do-it-yourself "pro" fake is an inspired example of youth overcoming its aversion to personal industry. ("We have to read *half* of *Heart of Darkness* by next Tuesday—and write responses?!" the students of America cry out.) It requires special paper, laminate pouches, laminator, magnetic strip encoder, a photograph that does not show the shoulders, even professional paper trimmers. (A few years ago, enterprising and well-organized undergraduates in upstate New York helped themselves to many of the above materials in their institution's Alumni Office.)

In addition to physical materials, the "pro"-level counterfeiter requires a license template from a peer-to-peer torrent site—a generally illegal file-sharing service that allows users to download files in the form of micro-fragments from a network of many shared computers. As the copied file comes from hundreds or thousands of sources, legal prosecution of torrent-site users has proved challenging. For a couple of years, until a senator complained to Apple about the absurdly easy falsification process, you could simply download the DriversEd.com app from the Apple store, and enter your picture and information into a template from one of the fifty states. Now, with the marginally less accessible torrent-procured template, you still simply change the photograph and relevant personal information using the official abbreviation list for eye and hair color (e.g. GR;

BRO). Aside from holography and state seals, that's all you'll need for the front.

The challenge is the barcode and magnetic strip on the back. An increasing number of bars and liquor stores check cards with scanners. In order for the fake to be "scanable," the counterfeiter has to generate a specific type of barcode and use magnetic strip encoder to "decode an existing [driver's license], edit info, program back into strip." Oh, that's all! I begin to see why "scanable" IDs are a premium commodity, even among the computer-native generations. The *pièce de résistance* of a truly fine fake is a hologram that goes beyond a purchased generic hologram. One must *create* a hologram, either by generating one oneself (math and comp sci majors) or creating a stencil with an elaborate and expensive scan/ photo paper/pigment process (the rest of us).

And that's not even for an *actual* professional fake.

The real professionals I located—via the Russian website that changes its name frequently, but has gone under carder.su and CRDclub.wu—recommend an even more rigorous process, detailed in "Ultimate Fake ID Guide V8." For this process, material costs are higher, requiring expensive UV inkjet cartridges and (non-handmade) custom state holograms. The holograms alone cost over one hundred USD, minimum order. Ultimate Fake ID Guide V8 is clearly a guide for people who "want to make $2,000 to $6,000 a month while staying anonymous and untraceable"—not even the most industrious do-it-yourselfer would tackle this project and make only his or her own license. The time, trouble, materials cost, and legal risk (making fake IDs is a felony) mean that few underagers choose the DIY option anymore, unless they are unwisely looking to establish themselves as their campus's fake-ID kingpins. For most college kids hunting for a fake license, buying is the way to go.

Buying in

My childhood friend Kelsey, who began school in New York City in 2001, tells me that she and her friends were getting "the *worst* fake IDs from 'photo centers' just off Times Square." Ostensibly centers for procuring passport photos and international student IDs, these shops made low-quality and low-tech licenses based on designs that had lower security standards. "New Jersey was phasing out their laminated paper licenses," Kelsey wrote me in an email. "So I got a plastic Florida one. All the bars uptown around Columbia accepted it." The photo centers weren't the only options for easy, low-risk fakes in Manhattan at the time. *Atlantic* reporter Adrienne LaFrance recalls a similar set up from the same era: "You could buy a fake ID by walking into a nondescript luggage store in midtown Manhattan and saying the word 'Arkansas.' Store employees would pull camera equipment out of a suitcase right there on display, photograph you in front of a blue fabric backdrop, type up a fake birthday and address *on a typewriter*, then laminate the thing on the spot." And did such licenses actually work?

Well, that depended on the venue. In Kelsey's case, some East Village bars did reject her. But she soon learned the value of confidence, nonchalance, and—let's face it—looks. A leggy beauty with thick hair and Danish genes, Kelsey always had a weekend fail-safe. When presented with "a pack of cute girls," "the Chelsea clubs didn't even bother with an ID check."

Another friend, Nick—a native New Yorker who witnessed two murders before age 5, and who fascinated me during my West Coast childhood by his matter-of-fact report that he took a taxi alone every morning to elementary school—tells me he got his first fake ID at age 14: "I chose Nicholas Flannigan as the name and Rhode Island as my residence"—but it was so suspect that he ended up using it sparingly. "My second ID was a very good one, though: a fake NY driver's license with my real name, address, DOB (except for the year of course). This kid Edi from school was the provider of this ID. He was very well connected." How so? "Albanian mafia, I think."

"Because I got Edi some extra customers, I only paid $100 for that ID," Nick noted. A good investment—especially given that it lasted him more than 2 years. And then, in a fatal move, he ordered beer at a New Jersey Nets game. "As I walked away, two guards approached me, asked for my ID and took it away. I was also ejected from the arena. That was the real loss there, since this was when the Nets actually won."

Which brings us to fake number three. Not even 6 months in, a bouncer seized it. The logic of seizing fakes is simple: no kid using a fake is going to call the police about her seized counterfeit (read: illegal) ID. Nick was left not only powerless, but also publicly displayed as such: his confiscated license ended up on the bar's "Wall of Shame." Nick wrote to me in an email, "So not only was I publicly humiliated in the moment by having the ID taken away, I was also shamed by being up on the Wall." The "Wall of Shame"—a board, wall, or glass-covered counter that displays confiscated fake IDs for the amusement of of-age (or successfully fraudulent) patrons—is a tried and true institution in bars that attract young people. The psychology is not that different from the shoplifting Wall of Shame in many Chinatown grocery markets: being a business's semi-permanent cautionary PSA is far worse than the momentary sting of being caught.

The legality of seizing fake IDs is murky. Most states direct that suspicious IDs be submitted to law enforcement; few bars comply. The most prudent bouncers simply return the fake IDs and tell the would-be drinkers to get lost. (Seizing someone's real ID, even when one mistakes it for a fake, is a punishable criminal offense.) The most shamelessly imprudent bouncers seize the fakes, then turn around and sell them on the street for good money. The Wall of Shame falls somewhere between these extremes. Not illegal but perhaps unethical, the Wall may put innocent people at risk of identity theft: many fake IDs are designed with real people's information, from names and birthdays to license numbers. The days of printing social security numbers on licenses are gone (yes, some states really did), but a license number in the wrong hands can be used to run an identity hack that could derail a person's life.

In short, the very existence of the Wall of Shame is a little shady. A legally dubious expression of over-age Schadenfreude toward the young and poorly supplied, it can be humiliating, and potentially harmful to innocent third parties whose information has been lifted for the counterfeits. And yet—who doesn't want to get a look at one? Even liquor stores generate positive online reviews for having a Wall of Shame as a bonus attraction. There's fun in seeing how bad the fakes are, how awful the plastic, color, print quality, photo. The sheer variety of driver's license designs is part of the charm. You'll see IDs from far-flung states, Canadian provinces, even overseas. In small college towns, you might see a familiar face in a photo. On top of that, you get to "people watch" among the licenses: Of all the people posted here, who's the most interesting? Who'd you most want to fuck? Whose photo is the worst? The Wall generates conversation about states, people, preferences, friends' fake IDs … and also a bit of drama. I knew a girl back in college who ran an impressively slick little heist to steal two seized IDs back for her ousted friends. I've heard of others stealing the best of the bad fakes from under the barman's nose—for use in the even sketchier dive bar down the way.

Or there's the option of retrieval via charm. That's how Nick's ID made it off the Wall. A friend of his, "well-liked at the bar," talked the staff into giving it back, then dropped it off with Nick's family's doorman. The doorman returned it—to Nick's mother.

I ask Nick about the form of ID more familiar to me in those days than the custom IDs he had: a government-issued driver's license from someone who bears some resemblance to the underage bearer. These, he agrees, were the more usual choice. His friends either bought them or, well, came across them: "If someone ever found a lost wallet, my friends hardly ever cared about the money or the credit cards. They cared about seeing if someone could use the license." My cousin Zoë, who attends a large university in the Midwest, tells me that the "real fake" tradition continues. She struck freshman gold and found hers in a parking lot: "I couldn't believe it— she was petite *and* brunette." O, Fortuna.

N.B. Those of us not in desperate need of a "fake" can simply slip a found license into a mailbox—the post office will return it to its owner.

Thirty years in the desert

Three decades have passed since Reagan signed the National Minimum Drinking Age Act. Everyone drinks less now, and drunk driving fatalities are also down, across all age groups—yet college students still binge with fervor: some 1,700 of them die from alcohol poisoning each year. More young people are attending college, which some researchers have found to be the most toxic drinking culture in America. The average yearly income of an American binge drinker exceeds $75,000; the average income of a noncollege graduate is under $30,000.

So what's the verdict on three decades of using photo identification to prohibit 18- to 21-year-olds from drinking?

Not surprisingly, the jury's hung. Public health researchers tend to uphold the existing law, arguing for stricter enforcement on college campuses.[3] Others disagree: over 100 college and university presidents have banded together in a nationwide push to repeal Reagan's bill. Called the Amethyst Initiative—an endearingly academic reference to the stone's mythic properties of protecting a person from drunkenness—they argue that a prohibition-like insistence on abstinence paradoxically creates a culture of clandestine and immoderate college drinking. Dr John McCardell, president emeritus of Middlebury College, kicked off the movement with a *New York Times* op-ed:

> To lawmakers: the 21-year-old drinking age is bad social policy and terrible law. It is astonishing that college students have thus far acquiesced in so egregious an abridgment of the age of majority [age 18, except for alcohol]. Unfortunately, this acquiescence has taken the form of binge drinking. Campuses have become, depending on the enthusiasm of local law enforcement, either arms of the law or havens from the law.
>
> Neither state is desirable.[4]

The Amethyst Initiative makes, or implies, an additional point: a law few follow undermines the credibility of the rule of law more generally—"By choosing to use fake IDs, students make ethical compromises that erode respect for the law."[5] The widespread use fake IDs undermines the legal underpinnings of civic life.

They have a point, but one could argue that willingness to act counter to legal statutes could be framed in terms of classic political activism. After all, this is the country in which Thoreau developed the idea of civil disobedience—the deliberate breaking of laws that contradict higher ideals of justice. "Law," he writes, "never made men a whit more just; and, by means of their respect for it, even the well-disposed are daily made the agents of injustice." I suspect that most college kids with a fake driver's license just want to get a buzz. I might even go so far as to bet that the majority of underage Americans—among them factory workers, students, military personnel, single parents, repeat offenders, death row inmates—have never even heard of Thoreau's idea of principled law-breaking. A pity: the young, an economically and therefore politically vulnerable group, might improve their lot through conscientious dissent. Consider the case of voting. At the start of the Vietnam War, the minimum age to vote was 21 in many states. Eighteen-year-olds were being drafted, sent to war, and killed in the name of democracy, but they were not permitted to cast a ballot. In 1971, as youth-led anti-war protests rocked the nation to its foundation, Congress passed Amendment XXVI to the US Constitution: 18-year-olds could vote.

The seeming triviality of drinking is part of the reason why the National Minimum Drinking Age Act has survived for so long. Why go to the trouble of protesting a low-stakes law that is easily transgressed? A law against teenagers voting means that teenagers do not vote; a law against teenagers drinking means that teenagers decide whether or not to break that law. The inherent value of "respecting the law" strikes me as dubious, but I do agree with the Amethyst Institute's broader point: drinking illegally is a more polarizing experience than drinking legally. The thinking often goes something like this: since I'm crossing a legal line to drink, I might as well *really* cross it. Social science has shown over and again that we seek consistency in how we view ourselves—we are driven to match our actions with our "self-concept." A self-concept that conflates drinking and transgression—*I'm-the-kind-of-person-who-buys-an-illegal-fake*—may indeed make it harder to identify with attitudes of moderate consumption (*I'm-the-kind-of-person-who-savors-a-wine-over-dinner*). Proponents of an over-18 drinking age argue that legalizing younger drinking may shift the nation's drinking toward moderation.

America, might you not look to the Mediterranean nations for once, and learn from them the art of unhurried and unharried enjoyment? A culture practised in true pleasure, in lieu of one that imposes Puritanical abstinence, strikes me, hedonist and pragmatist that I am, as the most elegant and practical solution to what really comes down to unforgivable tastelessness: red Solo cups sloshing with "Natty Light," Everclear Jell-O shots, Smirnoff-soaked tampons, vomit in the dormitory elevators.

Insecure

Youth will be youth, of course, and fun will be had. Lord knows I enjoyed my fair share of the usual college go-around. But my recollection is that many of us beginning college in 2001 were a little warier than students had been even the year before, more inclined to believe the cautionary tales circulating about ID fraud. In Chicago, my college town, simply possessing a counterfeit ID is a Class 4 felony. Like Nick's friends, many of us opted to use real, expired licenses from older friends or siblings—a less fraudulent, if more fallible way of faking our way into bars. Or safer, we'd stay in with vodka and some not-too-loud music. Even as we basked in the stupidities of Dionysian youth, it was hard to insulate oneself against the politics of fear.

But of course, the fear during that time wasn't all political cant, either. Fake driver's licenses played a direct role in the airplane hijackings and attacks on New York and Washington. The *9/11 Commission Report* says simply, "All but one of the 9/11 hijackers acquired some form of US identification document, some by fraud." But that understated "some by fraud" was enough. The driver's license would never be innocent again. "For terrorists, travel documents are as important as weapons," concludes the *Report*.

Once little more than a receipt stating that the *belle monde* of late Gilded-Age America had paid their automobile fee, the license suddenly symbolized the vulnerability and permeability of the United States of America—of *We the People*, of the world's most pervasive empire, of the planet's richest superpower. Driver's licenses were far too easy to come by, and gave their possessors access to many things, from bank accounts to airplanes; something had to be done. It became clear that the Department of Motor Vehicles of each state and territory would have to transition from verifying that an applicant was qualified to drive an automobile to also verifying that an applicant was *not* a national security threat.[6] This meant new processes, new training sessions, a newly emphasized role as the de facto "leading identity verifier in the country." The US security establishment continues to consider identity document screening as one of its most important imperatives. But how effective is this approach? Indeed, could it not be counterproductive to think in terms of gaining "security" from a forgeable document? What would it mean to "secure" a license?

"One of the games the younger TSA guys played," says Jason Edward Harrington apoplectically, "was kind of piggish." A former airport screener with Homeland Security's Travel Security Administration, Harrington burst into the national consciousness with his January 2014 *Politico* exposé on full-body scanners titled "Dear America, I Saw You Naked"—and subtitled, "And yes, we were laughing. Confessions of an ex-TSA agent."[7] Harrington, 32, left his native Chicago for a southern MFA program, and is currently writing a light-hearted memoir about working in the TSA while living with a colorful assortment of students, drunks and activists. I interviewed him on the phone; Harrington's laptop was on its last, unreliable gasp. Still, I could almost see us exchanging smirks when I responded, "Okay, now you *have* to tell me the game."

"Well, the Document Security Checker [the person who checks your ID at the front of the airport security line] would use the ID to note the age of an attractive female passenger, and all the other TSA guys would compete to guess her age. Sometimes it would be guessing whether she was 'of age' (over 18) or not. Or sometimes the DSC would signal her age and there'd be commentary, like, 'Can you believe she dresses like that at 51?'"

He pauses, then notes, "I don't think any of the TSA women did that with male passengers."

Document Security Checker wasn't a bad position. Harrington told me with enthusiasm about getting to see the designs of Danish and Japanese passports. (The inner pages of the Danish passport, I later learned, bear an interlacing pattern of medieval-looking snakes while a medieval Christ occupies the frontispiece. The Japanese passport had, for Harrington, an "anime" feel with its small, almost cute chrysanthemum icons on the photo page, handwritten-looking characters, and holographic film of Mt. Fuji.) Sometimes Harrington got to see American tribal IDs, sometimes papers from prisons explaining why a just-released passenger had no photo identification. Like a bouncer, he got to know the various properties of the IDs of America. "Some states fluoresce [under UV light] better than others. California and Virginia lit up really well."

"Did you ever spot a fake?" I asked.

"No," he said, almost reluctantly. But then he assured me that he and his colleagues would have missed *any* well-made counterfeit. An anecdote from Christopher Schaberg—an academic specializing in airport cultures and the co-editor of this book—supports Harrington's sense that security is more theater than rigor. Schaberg recalls that when he worked as an airline employee out of Bozeman, Montana, he had a running photo ID joke: "I had a tiny mug shot of Brad Pitt from *Fight Club* pasted over my own face on my airline ID—and got away with it [at airport security] for months and months. Not that I look remotely like Pitt; just that people didn't look very close—the semiotics of the airline IDs were all that mattered, dangling from elaborate lanyards and festooned with personalized touches."

"It's pretty ad hoc," Harrington tells me when I ask him about flying without an ID. "Sometimes someone would come in and say that she'd been to a party the night before and her purse was stolen and her ID was gone." Usually the person would have something with her name on it, though— a credit card, maybe, or a public library card found loose in the recesses of a backpack. If not, then the TSA supervisor would call up a national hotline and lead the passenger through a 20- or 30-minute questionnaire to verify his or her identity. Based on Harrington's account and my perusal of the recently leaked TSA screening guidelines, the best way to fly under a fake name seems to be to counterfeit an ID from one of the lower-tech states.

Bruce Schneier, a fellow skeptic, critiques the TSA from a more academic angle. One of the world's leading security technologists and a fellow at Harvard, Schneier has spent his career thinking like criminal. He can rattle off a dozen ways to bomb a plane. And thinking like a criminal, he is unfazed by the TSA's ID checks at airports. As long as it is not an obvious fake, he confirms, it will pass as real. Schneier believes that driver's licenses are never unfalsifiable: "No matter how unforgeable we make it, it will be forged. We can raise the price of forgery, but we can't make it impossible. [Enhanced] IDs will be forged."[8] And when they aren't forged, they can be bought. There's always a new DMV employee being arrested for selling "state"-issued licenses. The September 11 attackers bore at least two such licenses, one grand each, from a corrupt employee in Virginia.

Schneier argues that ID checks can only identify potential threats by profiling certain groups (with an enormous rate of false positives) or by matching a name to a watch list (e.g. the ballooning and ever legally dubious "No-Fly List"). His *Los Angeles Times* op-ed makes the case for a better allocation of security time and money, for, "in the end, the photo ID requirement is based on the myth that we can somehow correlate identity [ID] with intent [e.g., to blow up plane]. We can't. And instead of wasting money trying, we would be far safer as a nation if we invested in intelligence, investigation and emergency response—security measures that aren't based on a guess about a terrorist target or tactic."[9]

But *something* had to be done—at least, that was the thinking in the years immediately following September 11, 2001. So Congress came up with the Intelligence Reform and Terrorism Prevention Act of 2004, and George W. Bush signed it into law. In the section addressing the driver's license, the act called for the establishment of minimum standards for driver's licenses. Some states' licenses needed to be brought somewhere into the ballpark of twenty-first-century technology (ahem, New Jersey), and everyone was going to work together to make it happen. But just a year later, Congress overhauled this gradualist approach and replaced it with the muscular REAL ID Act. Penned by Jim Sensenbrenner, the Republican U.S. Representative who introduced the repressive USA PATRIOT Act back in October 2001, REAL ID strikes the same reactionary note as that earlier bill—even down to the hysterical *officialese* of the all-capital letters. In final form, REAL ID mandated two solutions to "enemy" infiltration in the "age of terror"—one, the elimination of legal obstacles to the construction of a massive wall at the US–Mexican border, and two, higher security standards for driver's license designs. To date, neither resolution has been fully executed.

Another slap in the face to states' self-management, REAL ID put the power squarely in the hands of the federal government: Homeland Security would determine the timeline and security standards for all licenses. The top-down treatment of the issue of driver's license reform, in some cases, alienated the very people who would implement the changes across the country—state governments and the directors of the nation's Departments of Motor Vehicles. These concerned parties—in the form of the National Governors Association, the National Conference of State Legislatures, and the American Association of Motor Vehicle Administrators—penned their own verdict on the bill in a considered and measured report, "The Real ID Act: National Impact Analysis" (2007). The figures did the damning. Eleven billion dollars, the price tag of simply *initiating* the REAL ID changes.[10]

This price comes not just from developing new licenses, but also from adding new employee training (e.g., on forgery and international identity documents) as well as overhauling standard procedures and database practices. The old practice had been to take an applicant's photograph after he or she passed the driver's license test. REAL ID mandates that all applicants be *immediately* photographed and that all photographs be archived. Law enforcement can (and does) search these stored photographs with facial recognition software, for wanted criminals. The ultimate idea is to create an interstate database system to aid law enforcement—which, Schneier argues, would be a disaster of incompatible and erroneous databases so vast that it would entail "enormous . . . security risks." Besides, the NSA has got us covered.

As with the top-down reforms mandated under Reagan's National Minimum Drinking Age Act, REAL ID has pitted the states against the feds. With Bartlebyian I'd-prefer-not-tos, states like Maine and Alaska, Kentucky and Massachusetts, have been holding out against REAL ID. There have been congressional attempts at repealing the law. With limited support and no built-in economic sanctions, compliance has been difficult to enforce. But a decade after its passage, after four delays to its implementation, REAL ID has gained traction. The law boasts a 70 percent compliance rate. The real deadline is when REAL ID–compliant IDs will be necessary to board a plane—which Homeland Security has set as sometime after 2016.

Outpacing the driver's license cons of the world is a Sisyphusian task. The insurmountable fact is, cons usually mobilize much more quickly than governmental organizations (here's looking at you, DMV). Like viruses, top-level cons rapidly respond to new security challenges with surprising flexibility. Shuttered websites appear under new names the next day, more complicated technologies are studied and duplicated, and the professional fake lives on. "Enhanced" licenses will most likely deter low-level identity theft and unsavory characters running across state lines to avoid child support and petty crimes. More elite criminals have had no problem keeping pace with the middle-of-the-pack states' license technologies; even the most sophisticated licenses ought not to be understood as counterfeit-proof.

Still, the security forces of the nation are willing to shoulder the burden (and pocket the funds?) of trying to outpace elite criminals. Founded in 2001, the Document Security Alliance, a public-private alliance that lobbies for government investments in the latest ID security technologies, works within Washington power structures to outpace national security threats (and spends money doing so). It emphasizes document quality and integrity as a means of combatting truly devastating crimes, from identity theft to acts of terror. The technologies possible through the companies that sit on its board (Unique ID codes based on DNA! Identity cards tied to authenticating pin-codes!) sound thrilling but are clearly too expensive for widespread public use. But face-matching technology was once unimaginable and now standard—who knows what other costly technologies will someday be sold to the taxpayers of America?

While the DSA limits itself to law enforcement and document design, another Washington organization, The Coalition for a Secure Driver's License, tackles social issues. It's dedicated to helping private Americans play their part in strengthening driver's license laws. More fundamentally, the CSDL aims to secure a place for driver's license security in the hearts of ordinary citizens. But how? How to get the Average Jane to care about keeping driver's licenses "secure"? Easy: make it about the kids. Oh, and get the message out by partnering with Boys and Girls Clubs across the country.

Admittedly, the CSDL does target pretty scary crimes. If an identity thief manages to procure a driver's license using a small child's social security number, he's on the fast lane to all sorts of bank fraud shenanigans that can go on for years without detection. The CSDL outreach advice to parents of small children isn't unsound, then: register your child with "the state motor vehicle agency record system" (DMV) by getting the child a government-issued ID card. Having done so we are assured, with a note of punctuational hysteria: "If an identity thief attempts to obtain a driver's license in your child's name—the motor vehicle representative will stop the transaction and report the attempted fraud!" (Unless, of course, the ID theft is going on behind the DMV counter, which does indeed happen.)

It's an easy win. No one's going to argue with protecting kids from criminals. But when the CSDL turns its sights to underage drinking, out spring the reactionary social politics. The organization's 2013 public memo, "The Societal Costs of Fake IDs," warns young people to be prepared to pay the price for fake IDs, a list of which is helpfully located in a box on the first page:

Criminal Record
Identity Theft
Serious Fines

Expulsion from College
Loss of Job/Potential Job
Alcoholism/Health Complications
Damage/Destruction of Reputation

At least five of the outcomes listed here, I would like to note, are a function of the *criminalization* of young adult drinking—not the drinking itself. The easiest way to help young people avoid these potentially devastating consequences of using a fake ID? First, lower the drinking age back to 18; the 18- to 21-year-old market base for fake IDs would collapse. Then address under-18 drinking via therapeutic, not punitive, means. Voilá—no one's life would be derailed by a permanent record.

The CSDL memo states repeatedly that underage people who use fake IDs should be prepared to pay the consequences. One of these supposed consequences is sexual assault. In a fallacious chain of pseudo-logic, the memo blames rape and the "destruction of reputation" on fake IDs: young women who have a fake ID drink; drunk women are more likely to be raped. Young men who have a fake ID drink; drunk men are more likely to rape. The memo's section heading on sexual violence reads: "Legal Consequences of Underage Drinking and Sexual Assault"—as if sexual assault would be of no concern without the *legal* ramifications of either (a) being a man and raping someone, or (b) being a victim who is found, post-rape, to have violated drinking laws.

Like an insane primer on why under-the-influence rape victims may not want to come forward, an explanation of the criminal consequences of underage drinking and fake IDs follows, directly and without explanation, the paragraphs on aggravated assault and rape.

Both in practice and in discourse, "license security" can be the justification for repressive and politically conservative agendas. One final example from the CSDL "Societal Costs of Fake IDs" memo: the cover picture, which depicts young people partying in a domestic setting. The credit simply reads "Image from NPR of an underage drinking party," but the photo, which ran on every major news site, is not a neutral stock photo. In fact, it was part of an attempt to discredit the 2014 Maryland gubernatorial candidate Doug Gansler, who was revealed to have turned a blind eye to teen drinking at his son's graduation party weekend. The CSDL specifically selected that image for its memo released during Gansler's campaign year. Even if it was not intended to be recognized by the memo's readers, the image certainly provides a clear marker of the attitudes behind the writing of the document.

There are interests at stake.

Syndicates

REAL ID has solidified the national trend away from homemade fake IDs. In the past decade, a significant amount of stateside fake ID enterprise, like so many American-targeted commodities, has been outsourced. "A friend of some guy I know" is no longer how all the kids find their fakes; the internet is. And the internet market for "novelty" American licenses has gone global.

Media reports about a new generation of fake IDs from China started surfacing around 2011. These fakes had the requisite holograms and watermarks, they scanned, they showed up under the TSA's ultraviolet lights in airport security. They were almost perfect, and they arrived in the international mail. These top-of-the-line Chinese-produced fake licenses required expensive equipment and technological expertise. The quality of the licenses alone betrays an extensive and well-connected network backing the process. What's the payoff? Not just the licenses' $150 price tag; it goes further than that. Online buyers, usually college students, provide the manufacturers delivery and payment information that can later be sold on the black market for the purposes of identity theft. Each fake ID sold, therefore, potentially generates two separate revenues—not a bad racket. College students, wising up to such cons, have started using bitcoin, an online currency characterized by public, but anonymous and irreversible, transactions. The potential problem with this arrangement? An anonymous seller who demands the irreversible payment first—and then fails to deliver the fake.

Of course, college buyers aren't a top-priority threat to public order. For US security agencies, college buyers make up the haystack that must be combed for the proverbial needle—that is, professional criminals seeking fake licenses. And a fake ID underlies a plethora of other criminal activities: fraudulent credit lines, bank fraud, insurance fraud, and so on. From a policing point of view, it makes sense to go after identity crimes at the root: the fake license.

Kevin Poulsen, an editor at *Wired* and one-time genius hacker on the run from the FBI, somehow accessed internal Secret Service documents central to a 5-year covert operation in which a deep-cover agent ran a fake ID business out of Nevada. To lure the clientele they would later target and arrest, Secret Service operatives demonstrated their capacity for a little irony[11]: they stole the identity of an identity thief. Posing digitally as "Celtic," a newly apprehended credit card con, Agent Mike Adams made fake IDs for other identity fraud criminals all over the world, gathering data about one major fraud syndicate based out of Russia. As Poulsen notes, using driver's licenses to hunt down identity criminals has the distinct advantage of tangibility. Unlike digitally traded stolen credit card information, a fake license is a real, tangible object sent from, and to, a real, physical address. "And," Poulsen adds, "being photo IDs, the customers had to provide their photos. It's a rare law enforcement operation that lets the cops collect mug shots before they've made a single arrest." The sting was successful, netting a total of thirty-nine defendants under one indictment, sixteen defendants in three more indictments—and the Secret Service's virtual storefront is not mentioned in any of the four indictments. To my layperson eyes, the operation skates precariously close to entrapment:

> One of the "overt acts" supporting a conspiracy charge against 48-year-old Thomas Lamb, for example, is that he "did knowingly and without lawful authority … cause others to traffic in and produce false identification documents, which were transported in the mail." Those documents were one of Celtic's counterfeit New York driver's licenses, and one of his $25 AT&T employee identification cards. It was Special Agent Adams who put them in the mail.

While Lamb and others await trial, and the Nevada prosecutor struggles to stay afloat under the weight of the cases and motions filed by defense teams, the targeted Russian ringleaders, and many other identified criminals outside the reach of US extradition agreements, presumably forge on.

Meanwhile, "scores" of government-sold fake licenses are still loose upon the world. The Secret Service let Agent Adams perform undercover identity crimes for *half a decade*. It did so, arguably, while knowing that nailing the Russian leadership was a long shot. It did so knowing the operation was unlikely to create any significant structural changes, and would only nab some minor characters in the ranks of identity crime. Why? The psychologist in me imagines an answer: sometimes it's not only about the drink or the crook; sometimes the thrill of faking is reward in itself.

Even for the "good guys."

3 DESIGN

Clean

"Good design makes for good function. Sometimes the American government just doesn't get that." From his studio in New York City, the young designer Robert Jencks vented his exasperation. "Driver's licenses don't have to be so goddam ugly!"

Jencks created his gorgeous series *Driver's License Redesign* while still in art school. In it, he reimagines the license, creating unified national design across states. His licenses are crisp, modern, and, alas, unofficial.

He repeats the idea that design facilitates, even creates, function, and points to US currency as a perfect example of missed function-enhancing design opportunities. In the US system, each denomination is the same color and same size. What wasted possibilities! Why not have a currency, like the Euro, that indicates denomination via its dimensions? The sight-impaired community would no doubt celebrate such a development. Plus, bills of differing size and color would eliminate confusion; I imagine far fewer arguments in shops over whether the buyer gave the cashier a ten or twenty. In addition to size and color, there's the matter of style, of course. The bright, unmuddled graphics of the Danish Krone inspired Jencks. He shows me a picture: "I wanted to do a license that felt like this."

He wanted a license that, by looking fresher, worked better.

"Okay, but tell me what's wrong *functionally* with the current licenses," I said.

He pulled out his license, not yet expired from his home state of Texas, and held it up to me. "You can hardly see the picture," he said. He was right. If photo verification is one of the license's main functions these days, then why was his image so small that matching the card with the bearer wasn't altogether easy? Moreover, the type layout was, infuriatingly, both cluttered and scattered. Since every state organizes the layout differently, out-of-state licenses require picking through a visual muddle.

Another illustration of the cross-country challenge of nonintuitive layouts comes from my Chicagoan friend Tatiana. When visiting a small liquor store in the deep South, she presented her card as requested. The cashier struggled to locate her date of birth. "I'm sorry, ma'am," he said. "I'm not used to foreign licenses."

Cluttered type layouts and state-by-state design heterogeneity may not be the end of the world, but they certainly don't facilitate things, either.

Jencks's redesigned license communicates its information clearly and quickly. It uses font size to guide the eye to important information. It has one image only: the face. No state motto, no "DMV" graphics, no golden seals. It resists photo doctoring by geometrically fragmenting and monochromatically recoloring the headshot. The effect is striking, and I can even imagine Jencks's license with the translucent holography, laser engraving, and microprinting that would allow it to meet the latest standards for government IDs. Here's the breakdown of Jencks's redesign.

Orientation and sizing. First, Jencks rotated the card to a vertical orientation. Type tends to work better on a vertical layout: from books to posters to newspaper columns, the eye is better trained to tall blocks, rather than scattered columns. The vertical orientation also gave Jencks room to expand the photograph; expanded, the face was much more visible and detailed, and Jencks found himself expanding further with each prototype. In his final version, the headshot fills practically the entire card. No "passing back" or handing down *this* license.

Photograph. Jencks did not simply put a typical photograph on the card. He created a geometrically fragmentized face, such that the image is formed entirely of triangular planes of varying sizes. The images' color palettes are bright and monochromatically shaded. In one, the shades vary along a plum spectrum, from rose to violet-blue. In another, lighter planes are a bright lime, with darker areas shading toward a rich teal.

Contrary to what one might expect, these abstractions do not efface an individual's distinctive facial contours; they emphasize them. The three-quarter headshots of the Jencks designs have the advantage of allowing more of the face's dimensionality to come across. People look more like themselves than in the typical front-facing shot. The argument for a front-facing photograph is that it can source data for law enforcement's new facial recognition software. Creating some sort of security lock over or within the fragmented photograph—embedded or superimposed "invisible" holography, microprinted details, laser-engraved contours—would allow a design like Jencks's to maintain the same security standards as the existing licenses.

Type. A thin white band tops the card, with the state in black type (all caps, a Futura-like black font). A thin dark band along the bottom specifies the essentials in large white caps: "5-11 GRN M." In extremely small print before each, category cues ("Hgt Eyes Sex") clarify without impeding. The photograph organizes the rest of the type. At the top, justified left and above the subject's hairline, is the name in large, clean white type. First line: first name. Second line: middle and last names. Third and fourth lines: address, in a smaller font. Important information is larger, less important information smaller. The remaining standard information is at the bottom of the license; Jencks pushed organ donation status and the driver's signature to the back of the card.

I ask Jencks about the official New York license redesign of 2013. Like many New Yorkers, he views it with something between disdain and unenthusiasm. I'm inclined to agree. The card, a new design from Canadian Bank Note Technologies, looks very similar to the Virginia license, also made by CBN: a white base over which are layered pale watermarks and intersecting microlines. The photograph is rendered in black and white, printed with an expensive laser inscription process. "It's hundreds and thousands of dollars for an inscriber," said one DMV official, commenting on the card's sheer expense as a key security measure.[1] The cost could possibly reveal more about the rumored reach of criminal syndicates in both China and Russia. Quality New York license fakes emerging on the market would indicate either inside jobs, or powerful, likely foreign, agents behind top-level identity fraud. Or everyone might just skip the bother and counterfeit New Jersey.

Toward the end of our conversation—night in Vienna, afternoon in New York—Jencks tells me that he has never been to Europe, but that he imagines it as a region more practised at integrating esthetics into daily life more consistently than in the United States. I mentally review the non-American touches of my own new life: the little silver-tone trays on which the coffeehouses deliver one's cup of coffee on a saucer; a doctor personally welcoming me into her a 12-foot-high-ceilinged office, and inviting me to step into a fresh kimono and slippers in her dressing room; the ten cloth hand towels hanging under nameplates in the washroom of my two-year-old's *Kindergarten*.

"It's hard to say," I tell him. "But sometimes I imagine so."

Invincible

But I have been unfair. Can we really blame America for favoring card security experts over artists and designers? As the highest profile country on the planet it is also, arguably, one of the highest profile targets. The knife hangs ever over its head. The Austrians can drive a car right up to the door of their Parliament; Americans have created sophisticated checkpoints on all the streets near Capitol Hill. In psychology's hierarchy of needs, the drive toward safety takes primacy over, say, the drive toward artistic self-expression. America is simply paralyzed in the safety-seeking stage.

But *what* technologically sophisticated paralysis, indeed! Radio signal and "smart card" chips emitting code, micro-holography, printed microcode, raised lettering, florescence, tamper-evident seals, laser-engraved photographs and secondary photographs in transparent windows, join more familiar elements: the state name topping an almost universally inelegant layout, the words "DRIVER LICENSE" or letters "d.l.," driver's license number, digital signature, the driver class, organ donation status symbol, even designations that allow the individual to carry one fewer card (e.g. "veteran," boating or hunting certified, etc.). Like a 1980s remote control, the license has more features than anyone knew we wanted—or needed. Holographed and bar-coded, tamper-proof, with a hidden state seal visible under the TSA black light boxes, with microprinting only visible under a powerful lens, with symbolic holographs such as

Michigan's loons, with whatever new thing the people over at the Document Security Administration are coming up with—with all those palimpsestic security elements, the 8.6 square inches of the license's front is made of a *More Is More* security approach—bureaucratic baroque, let's call it. But instead of the Baroque's frenzy for ornamentation for the sake of projecting confidence, we witness in the license a frenzy for ornamentation for the sake of invincibility.

Materially, at least, the license indeed prevails. Licenses have been retrieved more or less intact from fires, airplane crash sites, freeway shoulders, smoldering rubble. The license of a Georgetown professor killed along with her husband and two small daughters survived its September 11 impact at the Pentagon, and now lies in the archives of the Smithsonian. In violent tragedy, licenses are sometimes found before the bodies of the dead—the first confirming sign: we have an ID.

On the night of May 29, 1971, two South Dakota girls vanished en route to a high school party. The case ran cold. Over thirty years later, the state convicted, then acquitted, a man of their murders. In 2014, a fisherman noticed a wheel of what turned out to be a submerged 1960 Studebaker Lark. He remembered the case from 42 years earlier, and alerted authorities. The driver's license of one of the girls, Cheryl Miller, served to identify the human remains. Aside from a little embedded silt from decades in the creek, the license looked new.

Even for those of us whose unspectacular demises would be described by no one (else) as "violent tragedy," the license possesses a disconcerting semi-immortality. Once unlaminated paper, the plastic license now far outlasts its possessor. A human body will decay in, say, seven decades. Digital portraits likely will not fare much better, lost in the march of technological progress, obsolescence, and the sheer glut of digital data. In 100, 200, 500 years' time, the one physical, tangible image of your face most likely to have endured—in a landfill, under the rising seas, in a curiosity shop—is your license.

Bleak thought, that.

Estranged

The point is, though, that it didn't have to be like this. The American license—its form, its logic—could have had some other form, some other logic. It could be part of a state or federal taxation program, as it was at various points in the early twentieth century. It could have been a federally issued document, with uniform design and centralized national information databases, as is the case in virtually every other industrialized country in the world. It could have had a vertical orientation that doesn't have to do with being underage. It could have been a different size or shape. It could have featured different identifying information. And so on. Choices made decades ago have concretized into the American institutional logic of *how it is*. That's why it can be so fun to look elsewhere.

When my 20-something friend Sabine showed me her Austrian license, I almost didn't believe her. She was showing me an unlaminated pink paper about the size of a passport, folded in thirds like a triptych. The worn cover featured an "A" circled by stars, symbolizing Austria as an EU-member state. Loosely affixed inside was a photo-booth photo that Sabine told me she had taken herself.

"*That's* your driver's license?"

"Yes."

"Really?"

"Yes."

"But couldn't you just take out your photo and put someone else's inside?" I say.

"Why would I want to do that?"

"Well, not *you* yourself. Just theoretically."

"I don't understand," she says. "For what purpose?"

I mentally run through the usual American purposes. *Drinking*? No: teens drink here. *Airline terrorist attack*? No: you have to go through passport control for any major flight since Austria is only about the size of Missouri. *Employment as an immigrant*? No: a driver's license is not presented for new employment here as it is in the States. *Bank fraud*? Unlikely, given the tight reins placed on credit here.

"Helping a fugitive?" I offer.

She gives me a quizzical look.

The old pink paper licenses will be valid through year 2033.

Chinese driver's licenses may not look as unfamiliar as the old Austrian ones—they have the standard credit card shape that has come to dominate the world—but the procedures surrounding them can baffle the most seasoned expatriate. The combination of a thousand questions and convoluted translations tends to throw Westerners for a loop. True or False: "When there's a diversion traffic control on the expressway, a driver can stop by the side to wait instead of leaving out of the expressway, for continually running after the traffic control." This is one question NPR correspondent Frank Langfitt encountered during his three failed attempts to get a Chinese license.[2] "I don't know what that means," he writes, "but apparently under Chinese law, you can't do it."[3]

If the thrill in America is faking the license itself, the thrill in China is finding a way to fake the driver's license test. Langfitt reports: "Paying people to take your driver's test is common in smaller cities here. Authorities in Shanghai try to prevent it by putting cameras next to every computer. One of my Chinese friends got around that in western China, though, by aiming the camera at his face while a paid test-taker typed the correct answers on the computer just out of view."[4]

I had never before heard of cheating on the actual driving test. Did this kind of thing happen stateside, too? The closest match: a Harlem cheating scam that employed test-taking surrogates in the commercial license test.[5] Understandably more technical than the standard test, the commercial license test is a portal to jobs like *school bus driver*, *long-haul "big rig" trucker*, and *crane operator*—in short, jobs in which incompetence and lack of training might kill people. Dozens of defendants have been charged in the case, but the exact numbers of commercial drivers licensed through the scam is still unknown. Say your Hail Marys, New York drivers.

Back to China—where the de facto rule of the road, by the way, is "don't get hit." After three legitimate failed attempts to secure the license, Langfitt passed. How? He took the test, did not click the final "submit" button, and left the room. A paid associate later entered the room to fix the wrong answers. Fourth time's a charm, no?[6]

Eligibility for driver's license rules varies around the world. Brazil requires special training that teaches new drivers how to evade a moving carjacking. Switzerland, Germany, and Austria require full first-aid training. Many Northern European countries require night driving training.

Russian drivers must not be alcoholics, addicts, or suffer from mental illness. Memoirist Robert Osland explains, "[The first requirement of a license] is a visit to a … medical doctor's office that specializes only in driving permits. There is an ear and eye exam, color blindness test, and an obtrusive examination of mental fitness."[7] The good news is that one can get the license at 18 and never have to be tested again. Presumably the alcoholism sets in later. (The World Health Organization reports that in 2011, *per capita* Russian liquor consumption equaled sixty 700ml bottles of vodka, or around 2,400 shots.) In any case, my Russian friend Dima tells me that most of his fellow nationals deem it prudent to install a video camera on their dashboard to record any accidents for legal purposes. "You can find pretty dramatic car-crash footage from such devices online," he tells me. I decline to look.

In Saudi Arabia, women are not allowed to possess a driver's license or drive. But one "contented" American expat explains on a web forum that not driving "isn't a problem so much if you're married. There are taxis and many compounds have buses or drivers working for them. Women can even drive inside some compounds. Other than driving, the only other thing women can't do is go to some restaurants and shops. Well, they could, but it's not right."[8] On October 26, 2013, scores of Saudi women protested the oppressive law by going out collectively for a drive.

I ask my Iranian babysitter Behnaz, an accomplished linguist and doctoral student, about getting a license in her native Tehran. "Wait a moment," she says. "I'll show you mine." She rummages in her bag, pulls out the license. Even looking at the photo gives me a jolt of cultural dissonance. I'm used to seeing Behnaz with loose hair and a chic, almost Parisian personal style; in the photo, a black hijab tightly circles her face. The hijab is mandatory for the picture, she says, but she doubts a veil over the face would be permitted. For the other ID photo, her passport, she wanted to avoid such a stark effect of pale face/black hijab, so she wore a touch of blush and eye shadow. The authorities photoshopped it out. The resulting photo doesn't look like her at all, and officials at immigration and customs usually raise eyebrows at it.

Japanese license practices accommodate "cosplay" enthusiasts—people who present themselves as fictional characters from manga comic books or anime movies. The license photo must be taken in a police station, and must not include any hats or bright wigs. Permitted in photos: whimsical facial expressions, pigtails, a traditional warrior topknot, sailor outfits, military-esque costume jackets … basically any costume that doesn't block the head. The policemen tend to be male, the cosplayer photo-seekers, young women—though I found at least one instance of a charming male "schoolgirl." If I had to guess, I'd say the police enjoyed them all.

Age 18 is the typical global minimum for procuring a driver's license. Graduated licensing programs—whereby driving privileges come in stages for young drivers—may be found the Netherlands, Sweden, Norway, Latvia, Great Britain, France, Germany, and the United States. As far as my research shows, the youngest licensed drivers in the world are 13-year-olds who live on a Nebraskan farm and need to drive farm husbandry equipment to help the family. Agriculturally rich states such as Mississippi, Arkansas, Wyoming, Kansas, as well as the Canadian province Alberta, offer "Learner's Permits" starting at age 14. The standard learner's permit age of 15 still holds in most states. While the American minimum drinking age is the highest in the world, American minimum driving ages are among the lowest. Much of the world has the opposite policy: drinking first, driving at an older age. Some countries grant both activities at age 18—though not, of course, to be performed simultaneously.

Comparison invites speculation. Might the comparative minimum ages hint that between drinking and driving, driving is more essentially embedded in the everyday functions and social needs of American life? Or that in much of France, perhaps, wine would take primacy instead? An acquaintance of mine studied abroad in Marseilles during his sophomore year in high school. The French drinking age was 16 then. He was 15, but everyone read his birthday on his license (11/03/82) as *le 11 mars*, not November 3. Thus passing as 16, he went out every chance he could. He visited working-class bars, talked to anyone. And he returned to the States fluent. To this day he still speaks in a warm, southern-inflected French.

"If the license had spelled out the month of my birth," he said. "I would have had not only a very different time in France, but also a very different life."

History

As I said, the driver's license could have been something completely different. France introduced driver's licenses to Europe, and it was the French system of issuing every driver a nationally uniform *permit de conduir* that could have served as America's first license model. Some turn-of-the-century Americans argued for a national system of road rules and licensing, which by the 1910s even featured licenses with photos. Such a scheme was never realized. States just could not coordinate to create such a system. Rather than the simple and effective French model, early licensing and driving regulations in America ended up being far more entertainingly piecemeal. Thus, turning right on red was legal in Oregon for scores of decades before Maryland finally allowed it. In Vermont, you can veer over a double yellow line to pass a slower car. Montana won the hearts of many by eschewing an official speed limit for a few years in the 1990s. Louisiana allows drive-through frozen (alcoholic) daiquiri shops ("There's no open container violation if the straw isn't poked through the lid," explains my uncle who retired there). Mississippi—to give one final example of the heterogeneity of American driving laws—allows you to drink while driving, just so long as you don't get *drunk*. In retrospect, early attempts to standardize driving laws and licenses from state to stubborn state seem, well, delusionally sanguine about Americans' capacity for sensible consensus.

In the early days, circa 1900, when the car was a luxury for about one in 18,000 Americans—a vehicle for a joy ride, not the daily grind—a "driving license" was simply a yearly renewed certificate attesting to the fact that the state had been paid its annual fee for that vehicle. Essentially, the license was a scheme to generate more state revenue in the form of a luxury tax on automobiles. The license debuted as a fiscal document tied to a car. More than a century later, it has emerged a security identity document tied to a person.

The first *driver's* licenses were for the "paid operators" of motorcars for the turn-of-the-century's gilded society–robber barons. These chauffeurs were issued yearly licenses in the form of metal pins to be worn at all times when driving. Though these license-pins were typically dime sized and of a stamped lead-colored alloy, police were able to identify them visually. After all, these were the days when a motorist might complain about police laying speed traps out on country roads where a brisk "speed of twenty-five or thirty miles an hour is perfectly legitimate." When that particular complaint was written, in 1907, the limit was twenty. Chauffeur "licenses" continued to be issued in many states through mid-century in the same form of imprinted metal pins worn on caps or fixed to car interiors.

In 1910, Pennsylvania roused some class anxieties in its citizens when it introduced the notion of noncommercial licenses and enforced the rule that any driver except the car's owner had to wear a license-pin. Would these rich joyriders not be mistaken for, gasp, *chauffeurs*? But licenses afforded the state valuable extra revenue and kept tabs on motorists, so they remained in the Quaker state. The laws varied from state to state quite significantly, and guides were issued for those who "would be in the swim and own a motor car." Interstate commissions attempted to come up with "uniform motor vehicle" laws to reduce the confusion, but the dream of a national auto law never reached fruition.

Figuring it out themselves in true American style, the various states had their hits and misses in terms of figuring out licensing procedures. Consider New York. The new institution of driver testing occurred bimonthly on a main street of popular seaside destination Asbury Park. Not surprisingly, given the context, these tests proved more spectacle than anything. Sandwich boards were ostentatiously removed from the sidewalks of the stretch of road where testing occurred, blockades were set up. In the spectator area, old men assembled to offer unsolicited commentaries. Novice drivers being tested before the 200-odd spectators would show that they could move the car in basic ways. Panache and personality did not fail to count. Asked by her tester to perform one difficult turn, a young lady retorted, "Only a fool would make a turn here!" She received her license. During the after-test ceremony, she even received praise for her "horse sense." Meanwhile, the papers regularly reported pedestrian deaths from out-of-control vehicles. No automatic steering and antilock breaks in those days. Nor traffic laws. Owners of cars underwent no testing. One such new car owner swerved to avoid another car (again, no traffic laws), jumped a curb, and killed a year-old baby in her pram. He was charged with murder. Coupled with the problem of urban speed and anarchical roads, driving while drunk or chemically altered was a growing problem that didn't yet have a penalty. The drunk driver's license couldn't even be revoked in many cases—for car owners and their friends needed no personal license.

Finally, a New York Grand Jury advanced the notion that everyone save car owners should be required to be licensed. Sense at last, except when it came to the license renewal process. Imagine what would happen today if the DMV did most of its business on only *two days a year*. Now imagine that, but with everything *done by hand* by exhausted clerks. That's the system New York City once had. All vehicles had to be licensed by January 1, all drivers by July 1. When some foolish soul decided to eliminate the grace period after those dates, chaos ensued. On July 1, 1922, eleventh-hour renewal applicants swarmed the office. The crowd stretched on for blocks. Police—and then emergency backup forces—had to be summoned to maintain order. Racing to serve all weekend motorists, "the clerks were near exhaustion" reported the *New York Times*.[9] Imagine all the procrastinators in today's New York trying to cram into the DMV in a single day. … The crazy thing is, New York was one of the advanced states vis-à-vis licensing.

In the days of the Dust Bowl and Bonnie and Clyde, my grandfather, who later worked 364 days a year for decades as a fearsome traffic attorney in Dallas and Fort Worth, got his license at age 14 in the dirt-and-dust town of Mineral Wells, Texas. His motivation: "I wanted to drive my mother's car to the last day of my attendance in the seventh grade." In a lawyerly, typed letter that arrived in my Vienna mailbox one day, he explained the process.

My first driver's license was issued to me at a bank when I appeared for that purpose. There was no photo, and it did not mention race/ethnicity. It was printed on lightweight cardboard, and I don't believe the process of lamination had yet been developed. I took no driving examination or test.[10]

I had asked him about licenses and law enforcement. Did young people ever use fake IDs to drink? He responded that bootlegging was such an established tradition during Prohibition (1920 to 1933) that alcohol age laws were really a moot point.

> There was no drinking age as alcohol was illegal [when I got the license]. However, homemade beer was common, homemade wine was commonly made from wild grapes, and illicit whiskey was distilled and sold privately by bootleggers, and [even afterward] IDs were not necessary.[11]

If there's one thing to emphasize about this early era of driver's licensing, it's the informality. Sometimes a doctor's notes were needed to vouch for a prospective driver's "soundness of mind and body," sometimes not. Sometimes there were licensing tests, sometimes not. Sometimes all applicants got licensed, sometimes not. Even states that aimed for a standardized system whereby all drivers, even car owners, were tested and licensed, had a looseness to their regulations. The following anecdote from an online historical forum illustrates the attitudes of the era.

> My grandmother used to tell this story of how she got her first license in California in 1930. She learned to drive after she married my grandfather, and after work one day, he took her for her driving test. By the time it was their turn,

the examiner apparently just wanted to close up shop and go home for the day. So he asked my grandfather, "Can she drive?" My grandfather nodded, and the examiner gave my grandmother her license.[12]

I suspect that the procedural informalities of licensing held only for comfortably affluent white people. Informality can work as a discriminatory tool, too. The archives contain far fewer early photographic licenses with black faces than white faces—that is, of course, on top of the underlying structural disadvantages that would have precluded minorities and poor people from pursuing a car and license in the first place.

Between the license as luxury tax and security document came the golden age of American automotives. To follow the license across its history requires reimagining the great American love for what was once called "the child of the century," the automobile. It requires an historical imagination to feel the thrill of the new possibilities of traversing a continent-wide country. From both a practical and symbolic level, the American license cannot be considered apart from American Car Culture; an object cannot be understood outside of the systems of use within which it is embedded. In the mid century, when innocence and idealism ruled, when Joe DiMaggio was taking the plate and Marilyn was creating sensations, when the country still felt vast and powerful and young, the driver's license's systems of use included, well, *dreaming.*

The pursuit of — pursuit of

"So in America when the sun goes down and I sit on the old broken-down river pier watching the long, long skies over New Jersey and sense all that raw land that rolls in one unbelievable huge bulge over to the West Coast, and all that road going, and all the people dreaming in the immensity of it"—this is just the beginning of a sentence from Jack Kerouac's *On the Road*. The sentence rolls on and on, as if its length expressed the thousands of miles of road ahead. The love song to America is one of ranging, roving, heading west, finding the solitary self-defined against the immensity of territory.

The historical mythos underpinning America's car culture goes something like this: "We"[13] are a nation of strivers who have journeyed far to protect and pursue our core values, and now we have the right to chase our dreams. We have sought religious freedom (Pilgrims), entrepreneurial success (tobacco, cotton), economic independence (Boston Tea Party), self-governance in the face of "tyranny" (Founding Fathers, Confederates). We have driven wagons across a wild continent. We have built a railroad from ocean to ocean, we have inherited a world-conquering inevitability and exceptionalism called Manifest Destiny. We have built roads, we have homesteaded further and further from any help but our own resources. We have relied on our own wits and wiles and brawn to survive in territory without governmental presence. We have flown, we have fought, we have shot ourselves into space. We have dominated, in short, and we have done so by constant movement.

Car culture fits easily within this mythos of freedom and individualism. GM promotional material from the post-war era evokes the "American dream of freedom on wheels."[14] (This was around the same time the company bought up, then retired, all the country's streetcars, which were not publicly run, dealing a lasting blow to public transportation in this country.) The naming of American, or American-marketed, car models reflect the popular ideological mishmash of freedom, Western territory, domination, and space. Cherokee. Liberty. Wrangler. Navigator. Mountaineer. Dakota. TrailBlazer. Explorer. Expedition. Excursion. Commander. Freestar. Arcadia. Roadmaster. Silverado. Tahoe. Tracker. Sunfire. Equinox. Colorado. Canyon. Tucson. Patriot. The best-selling Coupe de Ville seems like a positively cosmopolitan exception, but it debuted back in 1949, when French names did not yet offend American patriotic sensibilities. But that's another story.

Car commercials are often prime examples of the vested linkage of *Americanness* and *cars*. Here's one: we hear a solitary fiddle playing a traditional-sounding tune as the camera shows us a young boy running to alert the Redcoats of an approaching attack. Suddenly three Dodge muscle cars charge through brush, with (anachronistic) fifty-star flags rippling behind them. We see a clenched-jawed George Washington leading the charge. Three men in three cars have scattered the well-prepared British battalion. Individuals taking a stand! In their cars! It's a brilliantly executed ad, and the clincher is the sentence-fragment tag line, the only thing spoken in the entire ad. A ruggedly masculine voice gives it to us straight: "Here's a couple of things America got right: cars and freedom."[15]

By almost any measure, the United States is *the* nation of cars. Despite the fact that a growing number of us may consider ourselves "poor," Americans own more cars per capita than any other country, except those havens of ultra-wealth, Monaco and Luxembourg. Oil is the most politically charged commodity in our market. Viewed from a progressive angle, oil motivates many of our wars.

How did we get here?

I choose to blame the 1950s. The post-war economic boom years saw the rise of two-car families in the suburban middle class. Workers, too, were able to buy cars for the first time. It was the age of *Fordism*, an economic policy whereby factory employees were paid well and could thus be active consumers in the marketplace. (Ford factory workers could, for instance, buy a Ford.) With money enough for mortgage payments, a booming baby population, and a mystifying obsession with lawns, Americans flocked to newly developed suburbs. With the rise of commuter culture, automakers soon targeted not only breadwinning patriarchs—stranded housewives, too, needed cars.

A 1955 Ford commercial features a housewife in apron and pearls, tidying her kitchen while chatting with the camera as if with a friendly visitor: "Like so many people these days, we live in the suburbs, and Dave needs the car every day for business. When he was gone, I was practically a prisoner in my own home." But now that she has a car, she enjoys "a whole new way of life": "I'm free to go anywhere, do anything, see anybody any time I want to." My mind, gutter-bound as always, immediately thinks of wifely mischief. In fact, the freedoms she references are of a good-housewife variety—daytime meetings with the other PTA mothers and leisurely trips to the grocer.

This script hints at the "buried, unspoken," and mad-dening isolation Betty Friedan painted so vividly 8 years later in her groundbreaking feminist work, *The Feminine Mystique*. "Each suburban wife struggled with it alone … a strange stirring, a sense of dissatisfaction, a yearning that women suffered in the middle of the twentieth century in the United States."[16] Friedan describes a complex set of social and historical factors, and proposes a feminist escape from the isolation of the suburban home. But Ford offers the housewives a simpler solution: "the fun and freedom" of her very own (hand-me-down) ranch wagon!

As the suburbs sprawled outward, President Eisenhower looked to Hitler's *Autobahn* as a model for effective trans-portation as the United States faced yet another global conflict—the Cold War. Fueled by fear of nuclear strikes, the United States broke precedent—large-scale transportation systems such as streetcars and trains had always been run by private companies—and took on the expense of building a massive interstate freeway system. The American government had committed to the interstate; the American people had committed to cars. Even the energy crisis of the 1970s did little to steer the country away from the path on which it was set: roads full of individuals making their way, alone.

Today, driving monopolizes US infrastructures to such an extent that *not* driving is not feasible for many Americans. The following exchange reportedly comes from California's Saturday classes for "moving violation offenders."

Q—California Department of Transportation:

What changes would occur in your lifestyle if you could no longer drive lawfully?

A—Driver: *I would be forced to drive unlawfully.*

Though certainly a glib comment from a bored Traffic School participant, the answer is also candid. The numbers are hard to gauge, but some estimates have it that most Americans with suspended licenses will drive anyway. For working-class drivers in areas without public transportation options, there can seem to be no alternatives. In fact, some people—on both the left and right—argue that driving should be a right, not a privilege (as the DMV would have it). One rationale holds that driving is such an economic necessity that withholding someone's license condemns them to poverty, and that, given this, we are owed the right to get in our cars and that elusive happiness. America seems too far down the road of its transportation dependency to turn around; "green" technologies or not, future generations of Americans will be just as enslaved to the car as we have been in the past.

That, or Teens might arrive to save the day.

4 TEEN

Rebel, fetish, chore

Ever youth-oriented, American culture tends to project its imagined futures into teen mythos. In the cultural imagination, driving is often a physical symbol of teenage individuation and newfound freedom. Depictions of driving culture capture representative teen archetypes across the decades—the rebel (James Dean), the corruptor (Travolta's "Greased Lightning"), the consumerist (Ferris Bueller), the risk-averse pragmatists (the prudent sister in *License to Drive*). And at the heart of this wild combination of hormones and pistons and exhaust and rubber, the driver's license: a key index of what it was and is to come of age in America.

1955. As the fast-driving, hard-living, psychically over-charged Jim Stark in *Rebel Without a Cause*, the iconic James Dean fights with knives, lashes out at his father, and plays "chicken" by driving straight into an abyss, leaping out at the last moment. He is all impulse and imprudence and rebellion and wrathful disillusionment. The film's character shades into Dean's iconic mythos: the young actor died in a car crash while speeding in preparation for a California car race. The self-destructive rebel smoldered with a nascent energy that later exploded into the countercultures of the subsequent decades.

By the 1980s, popular culture had largely downgraded the car from symbol (of freedom, wild energies, libidinous urges) to *status* symbol. Cue the consumer-driven teen, such as Les Anderson of *License to Drive*, a middle-class dreamer who "hasn't worked a day in [his] life," but who nonetheless dreams of owning a BMW and who ends up dating a Mercedes (the kind of girl who, were she a car, would indeed be a Mercedes). This teen type doesn't rebel, but rather embraces the capitalistic values of the rulers of the free world.

And what of teens and driving today? Given the lack of historical distance, that's tricky. With the digital revolution, new status symbols nudged the car from its pedestal. Urban villages and living "green" became hip. Parenting norms shifted toward ever more intensive supervision. Overt rebellion died as fear of the "small envelope" (read: college rejection letter) grew.

Let us look closer.

Every year the liberal arts college, Beloit, releases the internationally popular "Mindset List" about the incoming class of college freshmen. College staff invented the list in 1998 to give sympathetic perspective on each cohort's necessarily narrow historical horizons. Items include what notable people have been dead the kids' entire lives, what technology has always (or never) existed, what recent historical events fall into the historical haze of before-I-was-born, that sort of thing. The Class of 2017 list, for example, includes: "With GPS, they have never needed directions to get someplace, just an address." Class of 2016: "Genomes of living things have always been sequenced." 2015: "The only significant labor disputes in their lifetime have been in major league sports." 2014: "Woody Allen, whose heart has wanted what it wanted, has always been with Soon-Yi Previn." Class of 2013: "Salsa has always outsold ketchup." My class, 2005: "Thongs no longer come in pairs and slide between the toes."

And here's another one from the most recent list: "Rites of passage have more to do with having their own cell phone and Skype accounts than with getting a driver's license and car."

The statement holds, if not for a Skype account *per se*, then for access to social media more generally. Parents used to "ground" a teen by taking away car keys; now they take away the offender's smart phone and change the Wi-Fi password. Disallowing virtual connection in lieu of disallowing face-to-face interaction: this shift in punishment indexes the sea change of American youth culture in the wake of the technological revolution.

The car used to be the primary means of teenage connectivity. In the internet age, its significance has declined. Imagine a world in which there were two ways to connect to your friends: you call them on your family's landline, or you go to see them in person. Let's travel back in time—back before the next greatest app, back before mobile sites, before texting and sexting, penis pics on middle schoolers' phones, before Instagram, Pinterest, Twitter, Hulu, the iPhone, Facebook, Skype, YouTube, Napster, before AOL chat rooms, before Game Boys, before Oregon Trail, before CDs, before even the formal proposal for the internet. Back then: Atari was the video game system du jour. The original *Star Wars* was an unprecedented sensation. Neofuturist esthetics dominated much of cinema, with titles such as *Blade Runner, Back to the Future, Terminator*. Madonna was pretending to be touched for the very first time; Michael Jackson was debuting his glove and his moves.

Back then, no object was more fundamental to a teen boy's social status than the driver's license. Time never moved so slowly as the last quarter before Sweet Sixteen. From *Sixteen Candles* to *Clueless*, many of the classic teen movies focus on the sixteenth birthday. The 1980s hit show *Doogie Howser, M.D.*, begins with the teen genius taking his driver's test. Like the graduation night teen movie, the sixteenth birthday teen movie capitalizes on a potent coming-of-age event in the 1980s. The sixteenth birthday was the Christmas Morning of Adolescence, counted down to with restive impatience and impossible, acquisitive dreams of fantasy cars. "If you had access to a car like this, would you take it back right away? Neither would I," says Ferris Bueller, behind the wheel of a "borrowed" classic Ferrari.

Today, in contrast, young men and women feel more comfortable staying in the backseat. And not in the old-fashioned way: sex rates are way down, too.[1] Teens are just not getting licenses as frequently as they once did. Only 28 percent are licensed, down from about half in 1983. Each year sees a slight drop, according to Michael Sivak and Brandon Schoettle of the University of Michigan's Transportation Research Institute. Even teens who do want licenses typically don't rush out on their birthdays to get them.

This measureable decline in the priority status of the teen license seems to relate to a phenomenon of postponed entrance into full adulthood. Lest I read like the ritualized hand-wringers that have greeted youth from time immemorial, I aim for a purely descriptive mode in discussing this development. Who's to say that extended dependence is necessarily a bad thing? Here's what I know: colleges and universities have invented a new position of late, Dean of Parents, for the unprecedented numbers of parents calling in with concerns about their nominally adult children—and the nominally adult children seem to accept and solicit such parental interventions.[2] As many higher education commentators have noted, the presence of mobile phones on campuses has attenuated the individuation process that college once afforded. Moreover, my impression from almost 15 years in and around universities is that many students genuinely believe their parents can better manage their problems than they. (Confession: I once ranked among such believers.)

Accordingly, it is not uncommon for college students to call their parents multiple times a day—even five, six, seven short calls. Stanford professor Terry Castle writes of her reaction when she first learned of this frequent phoning home from her undergraduate students:

> "But when I was in school," I manage finally to gasp, "All we wanted to do was get *away* from our parents!" *"We never called our parents!" "We despised our parents!" "In fact,"* I splutter—and this is the showstopper—*"we only had one telephone in our whole dorm—in the hallway—for 50 people! If your parents called, you'd yell from your room, 'Tell them I'm not here!'"*

Castle continues: "After this last outburst, the students too look aghast."[3]

During a stint teaching at an American university, I encountered students still very much reliant on parents for everything from proofreading to contesting grades to solving interpersonal dilemmas. One anguished father flew in to meet with each of his daughter's instructors when a circumstantial depression compromised her schoolwork. His daughter—a sweet, underweight, childlike 20-year-old—was not present at these meetings. Professors, once sages, now find themselves therapists. One veteran professor told me that when she started teaching four decades ago she didn't need to have an ever-ready box of tissues in her office. Now she does. And not for seasonal colds.

It's hard to say exactly what happened. Baby boomers dismantled the authoritarian model of parenting and became their children's "best friends." Gen Xers invented time-intensive parenting and weren't afraid to question teachers' authority by contesting their children's Bs or Cs; the mobile phone gave kids instant 24/7 access to problem-solving adults; the threat of the college admissions process taught middle-class adolescents to toe the line; and overwrought network news crime reporting silenced the time-old "go play outside." At the college level, tuitions skyrocketed and, in light of the financial strain, parents and students—and business-minded university administrators—began to embrace a consumer model of the university, undercutting professorial decisions infelicitous to consumer satisfaction and success. The American middle class is shrinking. Business is America's most popular undergraduate major.

The license, teen car, and perhaps even the teen quest for independence have seen their heyday, and the new millennium is definitely not it. Fewer teens are getting driver's licenses now than ever before. The license, once a teenage fetish object, now ranks below a smart phone in terms of social indispensability.

Which is shocking when you think back a few short decades to the 1980s.

Talk about fetish object. In the 1988 pop classic *License to Drive*, car and license are metonymic for Teen Desire. The movie's underlying cultural assumption, which the script both reinforces and ironizes, is that the license is inextricably bound up in (male) teen sexual confidence and success. He who is licensed gets the girl. Starring "the two Coreys" (Corey Haim, Corey Feldman) and an almost criminally lovely Heather Graham, the movie follows the adventures of Les Anderson (Haim) in the days leading up to, and right after, his sixteenth birthday. His best friend Dean (Feldman) has just as much to lose from Anderson failing the driver's test as Anderson does; Anderson is his ticket out of the world of shame-faced and emasculating rides from parents. (Seen getting dropped off by Dean's mother at a party, the boys are taunted: "Hey dweebs, does Mommy hold your dicks when you piss?") The story begins in earnest when the celestially out-of-reach high school hottie (Graham) crashes into Anderson's world: she needs him to drive her around. Her name, provocatively, is Mercedes. As in, the license to drive might have as much to do with working her engine, so to speak, as a car's. Vroom-vroom.

By minute three of the opening, the movie has already invoked the fantasy of *Driving equals Sex and Adventure*. The opening track, Breakfast Club's cover of the McCartney-Lennon "Drive My Car," invokes an old blues euphemism for sex as driving one's partner's car: "Baby you can drive my car/Yes I'm gonna be a star/Baby you can drive my car/And maybe I love you": let's hope Lennon came up with these lines ironically.

Director Greg Beeman pairs this track with a literally nightmarish school bus ride in which the kids are shackled to the seats, which morphs into a high-octane car chase with

Mercedes in the passenger seat in semi-ironic reference to the Hollywood car-action genre. The chase ends with Les Anderson jolting awake at the conclusion of his driver's-ed class. Reality hits. And the reality is: he's nothing without a license. When he sees his dream girl Mercedes jumping into her boyfriend's convertible after school, Dean reassures him, "Anderson, the only difference between you and that greaseball is that he has a license and you don't." Which turns out to be true, as the long-coveted girlfriend of said greaseball goes out with him on a car-based adventure the very day he pretends to have passed his exam. Everything is made possible by entry into driving culture.

The movie clearly has fun playing on clichés of classic American car culture—rolling the car out of the garage while the parents are asleep, the overlook make-out spot, the 1950s-style drive-in restaurant with roller-skating waitresses, the challenge to drag race. Toward the climax of these adventures, Les decides to turn back, no longer willing to deal with the stress of driving the car stolen from his parents' garage without a license. Dean—not aware that Les never really got his license—fights this capitulation to prudence. With a patriotic flute piping the "Battle Hymn of the Republic" in the background, Dean delivers an inspired speech worthy of a presidential candidate.

You have worked really hard for that license in your wallet. I mean, you have had sixteen years of humiliation. Begging for lifts from people who don't give a shit about your image. You've had to stand and watch as all the pretty girls drove off in some older jerk's car. Humiliation— I know, I've been through it. But that's all over now. Les, that thing in your wallet, that's no ordinary piece of paper. That's a driver's license.[4]

At this point, he hits the climax of his speech. He punctuates his sentences with a clenched fist.

And it's not only a driver's license; it's an automobile license. And it's not only an automobile license; it is a license to live. A license to be free. To go wherever, whenever, and with whomever you choose.[5]

Sound familiar? The last sentence repeats almost *verbatim* the 1955 Ford ad from the previous chapter: "Now I'm free to go anywhere, do anything, see anybody any time I want to." And look at this from a current San Francisco driving tutor website: "Driving gives you the freedom to go where and when you want—confidently, safely, and conveniently!"[6] These repetitions are not direct references to each other; rather, they arise out of a discourse of freedom and driving diffused across American culture.

But what if millennials (or whatever they're now called) are on to something? What if driving *doesn't* give you freedom? What if we're stuck on the grid? Urban planners have determined that adding extra highway lanes doesn't help; with more lanes come more people who will choose to drive.

Driving is a trap and we're waiting in traffic, contributing to climate change—stuck.

While the French talk about the daily grind in terms of public transportation ("Métro, bulot, dodo"—subway, job, sleep), we Americans tend to complain about long work hours sandwiched by long commutes. Numerous studies show correlations between long commutes and divorce, back pain, sleep deprivation, and a host of other undesirable outcomes. A headline from *The Economist* says it all—"Commuting Makes You Unhappy."[7] True story: I once saw a man in a suit eating a bowl of cereal with a spoon while inching along Chicago's Interstate 290 during the morning rush hour. Inured to the standstill gridlock of traffic, he must have planned for it as his breakfast time. In Los Angeles, my friend Logan found a terrific job—completely opposite the city from her home. Her daily commute time that year: 3 hours minimum. One figure has it that Americans wasted "4.8 billion hours … in traffic jams in 2008 to the tune of 3.9 billion gallons of gas."[8] And money, too: Americans spend over 17 percent of their income on transportation. That translates into about $7,500 for an average household per year—money that could otherwise make the difference between eating or going hungry, paying rent or not. Call me commie, but consider this: if we Americans pooled all the money we spend yearly on private transportation, we'd have nearly $2.5 trillion. That's enough money to build the proposed California high-speed rail from San Francisco to Los Angeles—and *twenty-six* other comparatively ambitious projects.

When I lived on the San Francisco Bay, I was unwilling to do without a car. Without a car, I could not drive west into the hills see to the wildflowers in spring or, further, to the fish market in my favorite ocean town. I could not visit my two writer-farmer friends in wine country. Sure, the traffic was horrendous—but I was willing to brave it. My Buddhist chaplain friend from yoga teacher training once admitted to me that her favorite moments were hardly ever during designated spiritual practice, but rather when soaring along Highway 101 in the afternoon, taking in the ocean in her glossy white convertible. This is how the love of cars began in America: joy rides. American novelist Edith Wharton referred to a car trip as a "motor-flight," which suggests to me a joy, a liberation, a lark. Her less commercially successful friend Henry James would make her drive him for many hours straight when he visited his native America from England. I get it. Driving can be thrilling and liberating and everything we want it be. But it doesn't have the luster it once had. And maybe the young Twitterers and Smartphoners of the world are actually a truly sensible generation in recognizing that.

Social critics fret that today's young people languish online instead of pursuing jobs and licenses. In an influential *New York Times* op-ed, Todd and Victoria Buchholz called today's teens "The Go-Nowhere Generation" and worried that Generation Y is turning out to be "Generation Why-Bother." But maybe jobs and licenses and cars and all the hustle and bustle just don't serve. Arguably, what looks like apathy is actually the millennial sense that they don't want any more of the stress and strain of the world around them. They don't want to work a stupid mall job just to pay for car insurance so they can drive. They don't want to have to drive an ugly beater. A generation raised on Apple and sleek digital interfaces, they want more quality and simplicity in their lives. They want to get into college and be able to afford it, especially because they know that life can be difficult for young people just graduating from college. Global consumer capitalism and its sidekick, climate change, are creating crises no one can prevent. So who can really blame them for hunkering down in the dopamine haze of the screen?

The newly mainstream teen attitude of car-as-burden has moved closer to the radical left of the 1980s. In *License to Drive*, viewers see only one explicit countervoice to the popular narrative that car and license can end the dependence and humiliation of childhood. At a family dinner, Les Anderson's twin sister (wearing glasses, peace sign earrings, and a bohemian-style scarf as a headband) advances a progressive argument she gleaned from her politically conscious boyfriend: "Carl says that in America, people are misled to believe that a car represents freedom and individuality when in essence it is more oppressive than anything else, burdening the individual with such materialistic costs as—"

Les breaks in: "Wait—Who cares what your commie boyfriend thinks? I say it's great to be an American."

"I agree," pipes in the little brother.

The two brothers exchange a high five.

The scene is complicated. On the one hand, the writers clearly meant to satirize the brothers' kneejerk responses. The joke, of course, comes from the almost non sequitur idiocy underlying it (critical social thinking = communism; liking cars = American patriotism). On the other hand, the sister is portrayed as a nerdy goody two-shoes who gets her comeuppance when she's arrested at a political protest after trying to flee in fear. She's certainly not a dream girl like Mercedes, who wears a pink dress and heels, weighs nothing, and spends most of the movie passed out drunk. This hint of critique intrigues me: it's as if the social critique within the movie, like the social critique in the America of the 1980s, gets swallowed up by the dominant storyline. Despite imprudence and misjudgment, everything works out fine. Everyone has what they want.

Many poor kids don't get their licenses for a different reason than their wealthier counterparts: they can't. The family has no working car. The parent cannot spare the time away from work to teach the child to drive—or the money for driver's ed. The required proof of insurance for the license is out of reach financially; the rates would spike if the teen were added onto the plan. To live at or below the poverty line is to be chronically vulnerable to hunger or homelessness. One-fifth of American children are "food insecure," which, writes Jennifer Kirby, "means hungry." Thirty-eight percent of black children live in poverty; 35 percent of Hispanic kids. Food stamps are the only thing standing between another two million children and the poverty line. "Four out of five U.S. adults struggle with joblessness, near-poverty or reliance on welfare for at least parts of their lives."[9] For many of the nation's struggling families, driving is a luxury. Economically disadvantaged kids can't opt out of the license; they never had the option of opting in.

Rising poverty rates aside, the fact remains that many teens are opting out of driving. Are they rejecting the consumerism of the 1980s—or extending it to its logical conclusion? Have status symbols become less crassly materialistic, but no less status-conscious? For Les Anderson, who receives a BMW ball cap from his father and pores over car catalogs, a car brand—BMW—was the ultimate brand. For middle-class kids today, Harvard is the ultimate brand. Apple is the ultimate brand. They have lived their entire lives in a consumer culture saturated with mass-marketed "luxury" goods. Credit cards facilitate their parents' aspirational spending, and even working-class kids demand the "cool" brands. (A hairdresser once told me that she worked extra work hours for months just to be able to buy her middle-schooler top-of-the-line Nike basketball shoes.) Larissa Faw explains that driving anything less than a luxury car would be embarrassing for the entitled teens of her generation.[10] Then there is the aesthetic preferability of rejecting minivans, strip malls, parking lots, gas stations, traffic jams, driving school. The bus, metro, subway, El, whatever, provide a touch of street cred. One can lose oneself online while on the go. Green has an activist edge. Minimalism has been the abidingly cool aesthetic since the nineties.

But who cares? So what if the steadily growing teen rejection of driving is an ego-driven combination of status consciousness, environmentalist trendiness, technophilia, aesthetic preference, urbanism, and sheer exhaustion?

They're just stepping off the hamster wheel.

5 IDENTITY

The forged photo

"Licenses are supposed to tell people who we are—and they don't," the Swedish photorealist painter Fredrik Danger Säker was saying.

It was near midnight and he and I were speaking online from our respective studios—mine in Vienna, his in Stockholm. I had arranged this conversation to discuss his most internationally known shenanigan, forging his driver's license headshot with paint. It seemed both ironic and fitting that our conversation about representation and reality took place not in a real space, but rather via digital representations of ourselves.

"ID photos are thought to authenticate reality," he continued. "But they don't show how we move, what we look like in motion."

Säker was pointing out that ID photos—and IDs themselves—attest to a narrow set of markers and conditions. Ordinarily, we aren't posed straight on against a blank wall, in stillness. As Susan Sontag once wrote, "Life is a movie; death is a photograph."

Säker concedes, however, that his license might be "more true than other people's." And for good reason: his official driver's license photo is, in fact, a reproduction of a painstakingly photorealistic *painted* self-portrait.

Technical challenges drive Säker's work. "I always try to make paintings I don't think I can manage." Still, the driver's license project was the most ambitious he had ever undertaken.

The project relied on the fact that Sweden, unlike the United States, allows drivers to submit their own renewal photos by mail. The mission: submit a "fake" ID photo that will pass as real under the scrutiny of Swedish *Trafikverket* authorities.

The ginger-haired, 30-year-old Säker, raised in a small northern town whose only industry was a small-arms factory, tells me that the project took a long time to execute—100 hours or so for the painting alone.

The idea developed slowly in his mind as he fingered the old, fraying license in his pocket. Could he pull it off? The stakes were high—he didn't know precisely what the authorities would do if they discovered the photograph to be a fraud. He debated.

But of course he had to try. After all, "Danger" is his middle name. Literally. In what might be seen as Säker's first performative play with identity and bureaucracy, he presented himself at the local tax office one day to register his name change. He gave it to himself as a wry, but also accurate, addition to his surname, which means *safe*. I asked him if he had to show a photo ID at the tax office. "Actually, no. I just told them who I was"—and who he wanted to be.

In creating his real/fake ID, Säker's first order of business was figuring out how to create an authentically unflattering photo. To this end, he grew his facial hair out to stubble, mussed his hair, even tried to look a little hungover. He found an unflattering yellow-tone background like one might find in an old photo booth. He lit himself from above. Then he took a series of photographs from which he selected the seemingly most thoughtless and unartful.

He estimates it took him 100 hours to paint the photograph onto a canvas a little larger than 3 feet by 5 feet. He used a grid to orient his placement, but most of what this entailed was sitting back and seeing where he'd gotten it wrong.

"But—tell me—where did the finished painting not get it quite right?" I asked, genuinely unable to tell for myself. It seemed a dead ringer for the original photograph.

"I shouldn't tell you this," he said, and laughed. A pause. "Maybe my right eye."

But to everyone else the painting could not have been more accurate. His "photo" passed. Swedish authorities only learned of the prank after the story of Säker's license hit international media. To their credit, they responded with cautious support. (I can imagine certain arrest and criminal charges for a similar prank done for a US passport.) The Swedish position was basically that the image looks identical to a real identity photo, so it serves its intended function. Lesser artists, the official statement implied, would have been rejected.

Indistinguishable from any average license, Säker's changes meaning according to the viewer. To insiders, it indexes a significant slice of personal identity (vocation, technical ability, personality, relationship to authority …). To everyone else, it provides no more information than any other ID.

Säker drives a 1977 Pontiac Trans Am ("like the kind Burt Reynolds had"), but he mostly uses his license when buying alcohol. (Sweden has strict alcohol laws.) I ask him if any clerks have recognized him because of his famous license.

"No," he says. But a policewoman did, while questioning him about a current performance art piece. "I can't really talk about the piece yet," he tells me, but does admit that it might be "a little illegal."

So what's the point? What's the message? Is Säker's driver's license about asserting one's right to self-expression? Or is it just a witty technical exercise? Säker is loath to explain his art too extensively, but over the course of our conversation he told me that his family has been stalked by brain diseases—Alzheimer's, aneurysms, early death. At odd moments during his weeks painting the self-portrait, he found himself meditating on the idea that he might someday, or rather, *would* someday, lose the integrated self of his ID portrait. In the contest of the mind-in-control against the mind-that's-slipping, he would lose. His license, proof of masterly control, shores his immense talent against its inevitable, if distant, demise. His license: a *memento mori* for his present identity.

Though he predicts the license "photos" will sell less readily than his masterful landscapes, Säker plans to complete nine more paintings to be passed off as "real" and made into official licenses. He's on license number two. Painting someone else's "photo" presents a new set of challenges—the young female subject "didn't want to look bad" in an ID that will last a decade. She refused to let him use an unflattering photograph to paint. "Plus, she has such unbelievably smooth skin that it looks like a doll's. It's"—he repeats admiringly—"unbelievable."

"So I had to make her pores bigger."

This is not a person

The Treachery of Images. Chances are you've seen many reproductions of this celebrated painting by René Magritte. In it, a pipe floats above the warning, *This is not a pipe*— "Ceci n'est pas une pipe." Magritte's painting follows the spirit of early twentieth-century linguistics in cleaving the *signified* (the actual pipe that the painter presumably used as a model) to the *signifiers* (the pictorial pipe; the word *pipe*). The work's title suggests that the painted pipe treacherously invites us to mislabel it as the thing it represents. But it isn't an object to be filled with tobacco, lit, and smoked. It is a representation. It is paint.

Paint can be treacherous. But more treacherous in blurring lines is the photograph. "Is this you?" you might say one night, scrutinizing the long-expired teenage license your new lover has tacked beside the bathroom mirror. "Sure is," the lover might answer. "Or was, anyway." We might take a cue from Magritte and declare that the lover's photo *n'est pas une personne*. It is not, and was not, a person. It is a photographic representation, and in the Säker case, a representation of a representation. But the unconscious mind misses the memo. We don't always bother to distinguish linguistically between person and person-in-picture because on some level—in the signifying life of the subconscious—my image is I and I am my image.

And besides, the license may not be a *person*, but can easily be part of the ego. Our egos expand to take on certain objects close to us, objects that we identify as part of what joins us, *as us*, in negotiating our way through the world. Sometimes the ego has something at stake even in the documents of officialdom.

And just as the ego in a psychoanalytic model mediates between instinct and society, so too does the license. Indeed, the driver's license—both a control on and pass to the nighttime desires of the law-abiding classes—intriguingly mirrors the triumvirate of the psyche as delineated by psychoanalysis: *id* (urges and desires), *superego* (internalized social regulation and discipline), and *ego* (our "I" negotiating between id and superego.) In the ID as superego, the license reminds us of socialized and socializing controls on our behavior, from driving to flying to drinking. But within that ID also lurks the *id*, the Hyde in the Jekyll—the desiring and excessive self—driven to drink, to party, to see the strippers and get the lap dance. The ID regulates precisely what the *id* wants (speed, independence, sex, oblivion, risks). And the ego? "The poor ego," writes Freud, "has to serve three harsh masters ... the external world, the superego, and the id."[1] The ego lives, in other words, under the tyrannies of desire, suppression, and the oh-too-real *way-things-are* (taxes, death, the DMV). Moreover, the poor ego must also bear an internalized image of its aspirational self—the sexually successful, enviably high-status, radiantly fit *ego-ideal*—and it forever falls short of that vision.

Which brings me back to the license photo.

We aim to be gods of perfected orthodonture or face-illuminating highlights or expressions of masculine authority. Then we receive our photographs, see ourselves with demented expressions and washed-out color, saddest losers in the yearbook of life. Photographer Diane Arbus, famous for her almost callous images of freaks and misfits, discusses the camera's capacity to capture the gap between how we want to present ourselves and how we actually present ourselves: "Everybody has that thing where they need to look one way but they come out looking another way and that's what people [and cameras] observe. You see someone on the street and essentially what you notice about them is the flaw."[2]

These little failed efforts to put on a face: that the driver's license allows so little opportunity for us to put on a face is perhaps why we work so hard to negotiate even the smallest amount of wiggle room. We lie about weight and height. (A weight-loss T-shirt reads: "My goal weight is the weight on my driver's license.") Two anthropologists, Tony Falsetti and (the mysteriously initialed) P. Willey investigated the accuracy of self-reporting with the idea that physical data from the DMV could be accurate enough to help identify skeletal remains in forensic cases. No luck. Willey explained the findings: "People tended to round to an even digit. Every male was 6 foot. Hardly anybody was 5-11. One fella overreported his stature by 6 inches. And with weight they rounded down to the nearest 5 to 10 pounds," he said. "I certainly have."

"So what does a driver's license really tell you?" asked the press.

"That we're all very tall and very thin," said Falsetti.[3]

Falsetti doesn't understand this deception: "Why would someone, on this inconsequential document, a driver's license, want to distort their body image?"[4]

For one thing, anyone who asks such a question is an über-rationalist scientist-type who will never understand anything about how the rest of us live life. My father is like this, and I have long ago given up. Secondly, Professor, who wants to carry around an official card everywhere she goes with data starkly disproving her ego's mercifully softened picture of herself?

Philosophers often discuss self-deception in terms of intention or motivation: we want to believe something is true, we want something to be true, something is true (to us). Our official identities fit into the larger picture of how our egos manage self-perception. A Jewish Russian-American I know had always identified as "a tall, blond Jewish man." At Hillel events in college, he was always the fair-haired catch. But during his graduate school years, a North Carolina DMV employee disagreed. His hair was too dark to be labeled *blond*; Sergei, in turn, refused to be labeled as having *brown* hair. Finally, they consulted the list of possible entries, and settled on *sandy*. Being able to define who we are officially, even in the details, matters.

Who sees the license?

Just about anyone, really—bouncers, librarians, bankers, apartment rental people, those registering you for a gym membership. Lovers see it; lovers might even use it to retrieve a name lost to the champagne of the night before. My friend Margot confesses: "I personally have done the ol' check-the-wallet-the-next-day. One night down in Miami I ended up in a Suite at the Ritz with this captain I'd met during the yacht show. He was handsome—well, *super beefcake hot* is more like it—and his apparent nickname down on the docks was 'Hollywood.' … Besides going by Hollywood, he always goes by his middle name. The morning after, I *did* remember the middle name, for the record. But I couldn't for the life of me remember the rest of it. So I got up first and found his wallet out in the sitting room and checked his license and he was—swear to God—[*sexual- innuendo-laden name edited out for privacy reasons*]. I had spent a wild night with a [*sexual-innuendo-laden name*]!" It's a shame Margot won't let me print the name. It's great.

Like, *really* great.

And there it hides, in plain sight, an open secret, on his license.

Photoshoot

Perhaps concern for our egos—and our literal *self-image*—is why many of us dread and even rehearse for the one photograph that will dog us for years: the DMV headshot. Then again, perhaps you are one of those cool, laid-back people who, like my husband, wouldn't dream of caring about such a trivial matter. I won't comment on this indifference except to note that, between my husband and me, I have the better picture. Compulsiveness has its upsides.

And it turns out I'm in good company, in terms of compulsiveness. Scores of articles and blog posts advise readers on how to ace the DMV photo. A blog from *Forbes*, the business magazine, advises staying relaxed while waiting for the photo. Checking email (or, god forbid, one's stock portfolio) may lead to stress—and you want a relaxed, in-control look when you stand before the camera. Image consultant Ginger Burr discusses the right attitude for a flattering shot. Another image consultant recommends modifying one's makeup to account for the fluorescent lighting. Yet another recommends smiling as soon as you're called before the camera—you never know precisely when the shot will be taken. Still more DMV advice generally comes from blogs, young women, and other amateur sources, but I wasn't convinced that those tips would make a person photogenic. I wanted answers to my questions: Is there *really* a secret to a great license photo? Or is it just a matter of luck? When you can't control the lighting, photographer, angle, what *can* you do to raise your chances of a decent shot?

I wanted, in short, an expert.

Luck was on my side. I contacted Peter Hurley, a world-class headshot photographer. Fortuitous timing: he had gotten his license just a week earlier. Sure, he'd discuss DMV headshots with me.

Weathered and rugged, with a disarmingly relaxed demeanor, he tells me how he came to specialize in drawing out the photogeneity in his clients. "I'll try to make it short," he says, and his eyes crinkle with a flash of smile. Basically, as he tells it, his life has been a series of fortuitous and unanticipated events. It started with a postcollege job working on sailboats, which improbably and, again, fortuitously, led to his joining an elite sailing crew training for the Olympics. Scouted by a

Donna Karan representative one day while standing on the shore, he fell into professional modeling, posing for some of the best photographers in New York. A decade ago, he started shooting headshot portraits for his actor friends. Thus began another successful career: portraitist.

Photogeneity: not so much your looks as the charisma you project with your face and body in front of the camera. Hurley has made an international name for himself drawing out this charisma from his subjects. Sitting before a camera is a "place of vulnerability," Hurley notes, and often people react with an expression of fear. Many people's reactions to being photographed—perhaps especially after enduring a long wait at the DMV—are to retract the face and open the eyes wide. The result is a startled look and an indistinct jawline. Hurley shared his coaching tricks for eliminating this unflattering response.

For front-facing headshots like the DMV photo, Hurley has a maxim: "Forehead out and down." In other words, you move your face slightly forward toward the camera. From the side you'll look a touch turtle-ish, but in the resulting photo the face will be flatteringly larger relative to the body—and there will be no threat of an indistinct or double chin. Jawline is key: it slims and distinguishes.

Hurley also advises his clients in the technique of "squinching." His coinage refers to a technique of creating slight tension in the lower eyelids. Not a squint, it's rather a drawing up of the lower lids toward the pupil. Instead of the usual deer-in-headlights look of the unphotogenic masses, the "squinch" gives one the kind of cool of the Beautiful People. (Do an image search for Brad and Angie posing on red carpets and you'll see what I mean.) Hurley followed his own advice and did the squinch for his DMV photo. "Are you sure you want to look like that?" the DMV lady asked him. He assured her he did, and his photo looks like the photo of someone you'd want to get to know.

As more and more states ban smiling in driver's licenses, these subtle expressions that Hurley recommends give DMV photos some life and intrigue. They keep faces from appearing lifelessly empty. Today's impassive headshots make me nostalgic for the age when my friend Logan posed for her driver's license photo with a dramatic, quirky head-tilt, with the idea that it would help her get out of speeding tickets. To my amazement, it actually worked, even generating roadside chuckles from traffic officers.

I tell Hurley smiling is being banned in more and more states. He tells me it's a good rule: forced smiles often yield that goofy, "say cheese" effect that we've been instructed to produce since childhood. It's just embarrassing.

I agree. But it wasn't an aesthetic call on the part of the DMV.

No-smiling rules are being instituted because license photos are increasingly routed through facial recognition software and shared with law enforcement—and current versions of the software cannot analyze the biometrics of a smiling face. *Your face*, recorded and analyzed: not only does this technology ensure that one face does not have two identical licenses floating around in the world—it also gets passed along to law enforcement.

In 2013, the New Jersey Motor Vehicle Commission announced that facial recognition technology led to "the arrests of thirty-eight New Jersey drivers [for past crimes] … including a trucker who had been able to get three commercial driver's licenses under three different names, despite having his license suspended 64 times and being convicted of six DUIs. An additional 31 drivers were arrested for 'obtaining false driver's licenses' (without being charged for any past offences)."[5]

The irony is that while computer identification becomes easier, neutral-face rules may actually make human facial identification harder. Without glasses, without habitual facial expressions, corpse-faced persons in photographs may look much different than in everyday life. As one Texan commented on his new, non-smiling license photo: "I call [it] my 'morgue shot.' I had one TSA agent review it three or four times before she said, 'You look much better in person.'"

Covered

Over time, many people will see your license—but is this the same as seeing your *face*? That's one question in the ongoing debate over Muslim women wearing head coverings and, more dramatically, veils, in license photographs.

Sultaana LaKiana Myke Freeman, an American-born former Christian who converted to Islam in adulthood, wears a *niqab* and *burqua*: only her eyes show. Illinois has an explicit religious exemption policy for their license photos; when she lived there, she had no problem getting a license. Nor did she encounter difficulty when she moved to Florida in early 2001. After the September 11 attacks, however, she received a letter from the Florida Department of Highway Safety and Motor Vehicles stating that she must now have a license photo in which her entire face is visible. When she declined, her license was suspended. She sued.

The case brought up fraught questions: How far can religion reasonably extend before it infringes on broader civil society? Does "freedom of religion" mean "freedom to be exempt from civil laws and procedures"? In *The Impossibility of Religious Freedom*, law professor Winnifred Fallers Sullivan mounts the case that religious freedom—though "a taken-for-granted part of modern political identity in much of the world [and certainly] in the United States"— "is impossible to realize." By definition, there must be a demarcation between religious conviction on the one side, and secular practice on the other. Any such demarcation, however, has the potential to obstruct the full expression of some religious practice.

The American Civil Liberties Union (ACLU) took on the Freeman case. According to its summary, the ACLU's argument cited "three separate cases in Colorado, Indiana and Nebraska in which the courts ruled that individuals with certain clearly held religious beliefs have a right to obtain licenses without photographs. Those cases involved Christians who believe that the Second Commandment prohibits them from having their photographs taken."[6]

The case also argued that the driver's license was a document that had to do fundamentally with driving. It cited examples of non-photo Florida driver's permits (granted, say, to foreign nationals). Said Florida ACLU director Randall Marshall, "State officials should not be permitted to convert driver's licenses into mandatory universal identification cards."

A federal judge disagreed. Freeman lost her case, setting a new legal precedent. To my knowledge, no similar case has been mounted in the United States since.

Secular

A prime intersection between the state and the self, the driver's license has become an object of political protest in recent years—specifically, secular protest in response to license policies that allow religious headwear. In August 2013, Texas Tech sophomore Eddie Castillo succeeded in securing a license whose photo featured him exercising his religious freedom by wearing a colander on his head, referencing The Church of the Flying Spaghetti Monster, a religion founded in 2005 to satirize the so-called intelligent design taught alongside evolution in Kansas classrooms. Six months earlier, the New Jersey Motor Vehicle Commission summoned police when another young "Pastafarian" named Aaron Williams argued his case for religious freedom when employees refused to photograph him wearing the colander. Apparently, such matters require police intervention. Williams was photographed without his colander.

Researching these American cases led me back to my adopted city, Vienna, which conveniently for me turns out to be home to the original Pastafarian license holder, Niko Alm. Alm—once a music journalist, now head of a media group and founding member of a new Austrian political party—got his Pastafarian license in 2006.

A young-seeming man with cropped dark gray hair, he met me at the foot of the stairs of his office in an old-town section the city. He wore jeans and a fitted T-shirt, surprisingly "California casual" in the Viennese context. He invited me upstairs to sleek and minimalist offices in a high-ceilinged, pre-War building. We spoke in the kitchen over espresso. Staff members slipped through occasionally from the open-space office, intently nodding into their phones. It was fall of 2013, and elections were impending in Austria.

I ask Alm how he came up with the idea for the Pastafarian photo. For one thing, he tells me, he needed a new license. His old pink paper one was disintegrating (see "Design"). When he happened to come across the license photo guidelines, one rule stood out to him: headwear was not allowed, except for religious headwear. This blatant "religious exceptionalism" irked Alm. Why should religious people get to perform certain behaviors (i.e. wear headwear) forbidden to him as an atheist? Distinguishing himself from French models of *laïcité*, Alm does not want to ban *yarmulkes* and *hajibs*. He just thinks that if some people get to wear headwear in their license photos, then everyone should be allowed to.

To draw attention to the broader issues of religious exceptionalism (religious privileges, tax breaks, etc.), Alm had his license photo taken with an almost transparent colander on his head. As per normal procedure, he brought the photos to the police office and filed for a new license. Nothing happened for months. Then one day he was asked to consent to a mental evaluation with a state psychiatrist. Within moments of meeting, the psychiatrist, herself an atheist, could vouch for Alm's stability. The license was issued. Subsequent Austrian "Pastafarians" have followed in Alm's footsteps without ado.

I tell Alm about Aaron Williams, the unsuccessful Pastafarian back in New Jersey.

"You know, it's funny," he says. "The United States talks a lot about freedom of speech. We don't talk a lot about 'freedom' here in Austria; there aren't the same sort of expectations. Yet when it comes down to it, Austrians are the ones getting the Pastafarian licenses."

We wonder aloud about the gaps between civil liberties rhetoric and civil liberties practices in the United States and elsewhere; then it's time for me to go.

On my way out, I remember to confirm with Alm the logic behind the no-headwear rule. It impedes recognition, right? Precisely.

Two blocks from Alm's office, I pass a shop advertising photoshopping services for driver's license photos. *The before* and *after* shots reveal a woman whose wrinkles have magically vanished. She looks like a different person, like the non–chain smoking twin in an identical-twin comparison aimed at deterring smoking. A virtual facelift—talk about an impediment to unrecognizability.

I versus I-prime versus I-prime-prime versus ...

When I was a kid, we used to tell each other that no cell in our body remained the same after 7 years. Our bodies had entirely reconstituted with new cells. This playground wisdom isn't actually true—some neural cells endure until our death—but it points to one of the fundamental problems in metaphysics: personal identity over time. How is the 16-year-old who got the first license the "same" person as the 40-year-old renewing her license yet again?

Philosopher Trenton Merricks presents one classic illustration of the problem of personal identity, the so-called Ship of Theseus:

> A ship's old planks are replaced, one by one, by new planks. Eventually, that ship (as we might say) is composed of entirely new planks. But then the old planks are reassembled into a second ship. Which of the two

ships—the one composed of the new planks, or the one recently assembled out of the old planks—is identical with the original ship?[7]

In other words, is there ever a point that we have we changed so much that we are not ourselves? When is an identity document obsolete? My college friend Clarissa has an Arizona license that is valid until she is 65 years old. The best part, she wrote in an email to me: "It has a picture of me at 15½ on it that I am not obligated to change, ever." The worst part: before the days of ubiquitous ID scanning, new bouncers would occasionally get baffled by the 2046 expiration date and assume it was a fake.[8] The former Arizona policy raises the question—does personal identity expire?

"I can't go back to yesterday because I was a different person then," says Lewis Carroll's Alice. Clearly, we are not completely identical with our selves from yesterday. On a most basic level, we are physically different—new growth, new synapses, etc. On a psychic level, we are ever altered, too—not just after wonderland experiences like Alice's, but in everyday life, even as we think and remember the things that it seems we are always thinking and remembering. A thought's very reproduction introduces distortions and mutations. The neuroplastic mind thus plays a perpetual game of "Telephone" with itself across time. And so it is that we are never precisely as we have been, nor as we will ever be again. The question is, are these differences significant? Today-Alice uses the identity card of Yesterday-Alice. Do they then share an "identity"? Are they "identical"?

Clearly, some definitional clarity is in order. "Sameness of essential character in different instances," says the dictionary under the heading *identity*, from the Latin contraction of *idem et idem*: literally, "same and same." But—here my literary training kicks in—"the same" and "the same" are never, well, the same. As the literary philosopher Jacques Derrida reminded us, a repeated word is not the same in its repetition. There is such a thing as "sameness which is not identical."[9] Why? Because position in time (and space) matters to meaning. Meaning-making, or signification, comes not from sameness ($x = x$), then, but from difference ($x \neq y \neq z$). And also: $x \neq x'$. Position creates distinction. You never step in the same river twice.

Carroll anticipates Derrida as he plays with language, identity, and time. Alice's comment could be punctuated to emphasize the "I" as an unstable signifier. Its first usage could refer to the speaker, its second usage could refer to "I" as a word: "I (the person) can't go back to yesterday because 'I' (the word) then referred to someone different than it does now." Even at its most straightforward, the sentence gets at the central problem of personal identity: "The *I-of-now* can't go back to yesterday because the *I-of-then* was a different person."

A rose not a rose. Meredith Castile is different from Meredith Castile is different from Meredith Castile is different from Meredith Castile. I change; I am not the same as earlier versions of myself. Viewed in this light, the driver's license (as with other photographic identity documents) operates on a series of approximations. In practice, the license works fine across time. A decades-old license can (usually) still identify someone. Identification—putting a name to a face, say—does not imply equivalence, only correspondence. *Identification* document, not identity document.

The ID archives a past self with which to compare the present one. My handsomely muscular friend Hugo writes that, "My license now is from about ten years ago when I was a skinny vegan, so I get some questioning looks now when I show it at bars. And it's worth a good laugh when everyone's showing their licenses at cocktail parties."

I've been gesturing toward a theory of identity in which identity (equivalence) is impossible. But what of continuity? Surely the skinny vegan and the hunky man are more similar than different. Many philosophers (and likely all theologians) would argue that while personal identity changes over time, a certain *something* cuts across time. Personality, memory, experience. Essence, aura, soul. A core component that is, at least temporarily, transcendent.

My own current driver's license shows a California address, 6,000 miles from where I live today. At the moment the photo was taken, my then-husband stood behind the camera, bent over a Canetti novel. I remember: my eye had just flitted back to the camera from his face.

During our divorce, I studied my license photo as if it were a riddle I needed to solve. I sat in the wide, high windowsill of a Berlin kitchen, tree-crown level, and stared at the card in my hands, trying to make sense of that little scene of ordinary life: husband, wife, errand at the DMV, waiting, reading, my glance up, his eyes down.

In the photo, behind my closed-lipped smile, my jaw is visibly clenched. My hair is longer and wilder than it is now. My skin is browned from a summer in meadows, eyes hold back; an expression almost aggressive in its neutrality. But then the chin tilts slightly up, as if in—what?—triumph? Arrogance? Toughness?

But it was no good: I had forgotten. I could not feel it inside, nor could I read it from without. The husband, the jawline, the wide yet closed face. Studying it, I discerned nothing.

"It's a good picture," the DMV woman had said with gruff goodwill.

"May I see it?"

Her official character clicked in. "You'll see it on your license in a week or two."

And she moved on to the next person in line.

For most of us, significant life changes are not reflected in the driver's license. My next driver's license will show some fine lines, but will say nothing directly of a divorce, degree, expatriation, a love, a child, a newspaper job, this book. The bureaucratic markers of time—the license photo, the passport photo—are often most interesting when they do not correspond with the momentous events of life. Here was another more or less ordinary day, exceptional only in that I had to take the time to present myself for a bureaucratic ID picture.

But there's one identity marker on which the license is not mute: sex—or rather, a sex *change*. No one has a more obvious disjuncture between licenses than a person who has transitioned from one gender to the other. And no one is more endangered by the lag between identity and license.

Outed

"When is an ID not an ID?" said Lisa Mottet, on the phone with me from Washington, D.C. "When it becomes a transsexual outing card."

Mottet, a Georgetown-trained lawyer and the Deputy Executive Director at the National Center for Transgender Equality, advocates for, among other things, more progressive driver's license policies in all fifty states.[10] She sees the driver's license as an object that can either put transsexuals in danger or socially confirm their gender expression.

A license that matches gender to the bearer's self-presentation is necessary for an unfettered life in the United States. Female transsexuals often encounter suspicion and mistrust in public restrooms; an ID with correct gender confirmation can prevent a scene or a call to security.

On the other hand, gender inconsistencies between bearer and license (name, appearance, designated sex) make transsexual people vulnerable to harassment, discrimination, and violence. It robs them of their discretion and indiscriminately reveals their "official" sex to anyone who inspects their IDs, from traffic police to nosy acquaintances to employers. In the influential 1999 movie *Boys Don't Cry,* based on the 1993 rape and murder of a transsexual man in Nebraska, the main character has to use a fake ID to protect himself from detection.

America can be a dangerous place for transsexual people. Let's review 2013, the last year for which complete data is available: fifteen *reported* murders of transsexuals in the United States—an average year. Given law enforcement's tendency to default to the birth gender and to pass over trans-sexuality in silence, the number is likely higher. In August, the young transsexual Islan Nettles was beaten to death directly across the street from a Harlem police station. Police pulled her assailant off her and to date, he walks free. Just weeks earlier, another transsexual woman, Diamond Williams, was killed and dismembered with an axe in Philadelphia. In the spring of 2013, Cemia Dove Acoff was found naked from the waist down in a pond, the first of three transsexuals murdered in Cleveland that year. At the beginning of the year, January 1, in Milwaukee, a 22-year-old transsexual man and rapper named Evon Young was singled out as the victim of a gang initiation murder. This was no shooting; he was chained by the neck, choked with plastic, and beaten with tools. It wasn't incidental that he was transsexual.

In short, transsexuals in America not only live in fear of death, but of death by wretched, hateful means. Then there is the potentially chronic, even systemic discrimination, ranging from abusive comments on the street to rejection by relatives, from workplace harassment to chronic underemployment despite qualifications.

As if that's not enough, often the DMV is another frustrating obstacle in transsexuals' lives. Psychiatric documentation of the transsexual's status must be provided. A name change with Social Security validation may be a requirement. The DMV also usually wants proof of progress toward full gender reassignment, such as hormone therapy. Mottet tells me that around ten states still require proof that the individual has had surgery. This is outrageous in three ways: (1) not all transsexuals find surgery necessary, (2) it is a gross violation of privacy to require medical records, and (3) the cost of surgery many transsexuals opt for—sex reassignment surgery—is about a quarter of a million dollars and almost never covered by insurance. An Alaskan transsexual recently won a suit arguing point number two above (medical privacy), which may strengthen the momentum toward fairer and more explicit laws. It's a push in the right direction, after a difficult decade or so. Transsexuals were hit hard, after September 11, 2001, when loosely run DMVs that previously would change the gender marker without question, became more inflexible. Throughout it all, though, Mottet says, there are employees in a number of states known to the transsexual community to be sympathetic and willing to push the gender change through.

And then there are the jerks. In 2011, a California DMV employee sent a transsexual patron a letter about "abomination" leading to hell.[11] That same year, a prominent Florida transsexual, Victoria Michaels Lavelle, waited in line for hours during her four attempts to change her gender marker, which would have required a simple click of a mouse by any DMV clerk. Moreover, clerks treated her rudely and loudly "outed" her to the many waiting patrons.[12]

One of the more troublesome aspects of transsexual discrimination in the United States is that often police are often the source of harassment, rather than protection against it. Mottet gives me an example of a transsexual woman who was stopped for a broken taillight, then detained at the side of the road for forty minutes when the officer saw that she was identified as "male" on her license. Then there was the case of Rachel Fantelli, a transsexual off-road racer who attracted the notice of federal agents while doing a photo shoot on isolated public land. The agents asked for the group's IDs; Rachel's ID still showed her as being a man. "He was super nice until he saw the ID," Fantelli told the *San Diego Union-Tribune*. "He went from calling me 'Miss' and 'Ma'am' when it first started, to 'Sir,' 'Dude' and eventually … 'it.'" Then the agent tasered the unresisting Fantelli in the belly and, while she lay on the ground, on her genitals.

But Mottet surprised me by saying that one of the most corrosive effects of regressive DMV gender policies is that transsexuals end up retreating from full participation in society. With an ID that might out them, bars are not safe, streets are not safe, airports are not safe. And, unsafe, transsexuals cannot thrive. Mottet told me that just the month prior, she received an email from a Maryland teenager whose frustration and despair were palpable through the screen. "I feel at my last limb," he wrote. The 17-year-old transsexual man described how he felt trapped in his suburban home. He wanted to find a job and secure more independence, but he feared that an "F" license would expose him to employers. With *pro bono* legal aid and documentation from a psychiatric social worker, the young man was able to secure a license that read "M." Finally he could begin his life.

"What would be the most progressive approach to driver's licenses from a sex/gender perspective?" I asked Mottet.

"One idea is to leave sex off the license," she said.

My mind rebelled. Gender is the primary identity marker with which most of us sort the people around us. Few of us are content to leave androgynous people unsorted. *Man or woman?* the rigid little mental computer asks, gathering what data it can. The question new parents most often encounter: *Boy or girl?* How could an identity document not cater to such heavily socialized gender primacy?

Actually, it'd be fairly feasible. Physical identity markers such as a photo, height, and eye color are sufficient to identify a person. The driver's name, bar code, and birth date make digital database sorting possible without needing the gender field. Or: gender could be coded within the driver's license number, available to authorities but less obvious to lay eyes. If the social security card can survive without gender, surely so, too, can the driver's license.

America might take comfort in the knowledge that the license has already survived the loss of many identity categories. Consider the 1938 license of Oakland, California resident Margaret Beatrice Kyle of 537 Lewis St. In white type on glossy, textured black paper, we learn that Miss Kyle is female, unmarried, 5-3½ and 147½, 21 years old (the math is done for us). Her date of birth is September 20, 1916. There is a blurry right thumb-print; there is no photograph. Her "Color Eyes," a lower-case *brown*; her "Color Hair," a lower-case *black*. Her "Race," an upper-case *Colored*. Race was once as reified and as essentialized a biological category as gender is now. French intellectual historian Michel Foucault famously argued that seemingly natural categories in fact conceal power relations; remove the identity category and you drain it of its power. And if you can't change the categories, then let the document *not* have the final word. Foucault: "I am no doubt not the only one who writes in order to have no face. Do not ask who I am and do not ask me to remain the same: leave it to our bureaucrats and our police to see that our papers are in order."[13]

An extrapolation: the category "Identity" itself may no longer serve.

6 CIVICS

Here follow four brief sketches of emerging issues for the American license: surveillance, suspension, voting, and undocumented immigrants. It is no sooner typed than it is historic—politics and technology spin on, unstopping. But the details don't matter. The fundamental ideological problems of how the license regulates (or not) the civic lives of its citizens: these abide. America will continue to grapple with how to shape and organize and, more ominously, control participation in national civic life. We will continue to debate the relative merits of pragmatism versus idealism in dealing with inconvenient realities such as the large number of unlicensed immigrant drivers, or the millions of cash-strapped Americans driving on suspended licenses. And America will continue to weigh the sacrifice of personal privacy against the benefits of a highly regulated and surveilled civic life.

Remotely yours, xoxo, America

The future is here: Radio Frequency Identification has entered the world of the driver's license. A radio device embedded within the license allows police—or anyone with a reader (on sale from about $50)—to track the unique ID reference numbers of licenses up to fifty meters away.[1] Simply enter the reference numbers into the Department of Homeland Security database, and—bing!—up pops all the biographical and biometric information from a scanned license. For this step, even the non-hackers of the world could presumably find a cop to bribe.

The bottom line: "If you carry one of these licenses in your wallet or purse, you can be tracked and stalked without your knowledge or consent."[2]

Originally designed for manufacturers to track objects' whereabouts, RFID technologies are now used to track people, monitor behavior, unlock doors, analyze inventory. According to an industry report, both Wal-Mart and the US Department of Defense "have mandated that their top suppliers deploy RFID."[3] Encrypted RFID is now used in passports and credit cards. Pfizer tracks its drugs with it. Fido and Felix, and Hamburger and Swine, are microchipped with it. Tires and T-shirts and handbags and shoes have them. VIP beach bar guests not willing to carry a credit card with their swimwear can get RFID chips embedded under their skin with a thick syringe (presumably, after consuming a few drinks?). Dorms and laboratories use RFID cards to unlock doors, Prius autos use them as engine "keys," hospitals use them to monitor employee hand washing, screen patients, and cue time-released pharmaceuticals. Surely the NSA et al. have spied with it. "Some RFID tags are thin enough to be embedded in paper," reports an industry newsletter.[4] Large-currency bills have not yet, but could be, embedded with tags. The current smallest tags come in powder form. Edible RFID inks also exist, for the benefit of big agribusiness.

Given the proliferation of these radio IDs, is their use in licenses alarming? It depends. Radio frequency IDs are not secure, as a number of security experts independently demonstrated in 2006. Security technologist Jonathan Westhues hacked into and cloned a supposedly counterfeit-proof RFID before a live conference audience; Steven Boggan of the *Guardian* teamed up with a privacy expert to hack into new RFIDs in British passports; Dutch researchers came up with a way to infect RFID devices with viruses; and the European Union's Future of Identity in the Information Society (Fidis) announced that RFID documents were "poorly conceived" and that they "dramatically decrease [citizens'] security and privacy, and increase [the] risk of identity theft."[5] Subsequent upgrades of radio ID technology have likewise proved vulnerable to attack.

On the basis of such vulnerabilities, the Enhanced Driver's License, as Homeland Security calls licenses with RFID, links only to a reference number, no other information. This reference number is then used to retrieve the driver's information from a secure Department of Homeland Security database. Third parties seem less a problem, then, than potential "legitimate" government surveillance.

The United States government has invested dearly in the remote surveillance of its citizens via driver's licenses

(Remember REAL ID's 11 billion dollar minimum price tag?), and precedent suggests that it will continue to invest in new license technology. Just as wars are being fought remotely via drones and ultra–long range bullets, policing seems to be going remote as well. License technology is certainly not "there" yet; its range is far too limited. (Better to track citizens via mobile networks.) Unlike "active" radio ID systems like E-ZPass toll road devices, the passive RFID in licenses must receive its charge from electrons emitted by special electronic readers. But soon, more remote radio tracking could be used in the driver's license. The technology is here, or almost here. Moreover, market demand could drive prices down for active tags. From there, it's just one short leap to, "Well, this new technology doesn't cost much more money *and* it will keep America safer...."

RFID may or may not be sinister, but what *is* sinister is how little information people are given when they receive an "enhanced" license—it is billed as a travel option, not a policing option. Washington State's DMV equivalent, the Department of Licensing, explains its rationale for offering this new enhanced card. It mentions nothing of RFID's domestic use.

> The federal government recently passed the Western Hemisphere Travel Initiative (WHTI), which requires a passport or other federally-approved identification or proof-of-citizenship document for all travel into the United States. To preserve travel, trade, and cultural ties

with British Columbia and increase security at the border, we are offering EDL/EID [Enhanced Driver's License/ Enhanced ID] Cards to Washington residents who choose to participate. The EDL/EID meets federal requirements, and is an approved alternative to a passport for re-entry into the U.S at land and sea borders between the U.S., Canada, Mexico, Bermuda, and the Caribbean.[6]

A naïve reader might conclude that the card saves you money on a passport, that's all.

RFIDs work by allowing police to enter individual license holders on a watch list. These drivers may be individuals with criminal records or moving violations, or they may simply be random citizens under surveillance. When police detect flagged IDs, cars are much more likely to be pulled over. But never fear: should you someday find yourself an object of police interest, stopped regularly for questioning, the home cure is, reportedly, simple.[7] One evader reported online that microwaving her license for ten seconds solved her problem of constant police apprehension. Other ideas include simple foil shields that prevent electronic readers from detecting the card.

There has also been talk of hammers.

Suspensions

Young drivers without valid licenses play a role in nearly half of fatal crashes—48.8 percent.[8] For 2013, that's over

17,000 funerals. Yearly, about 7,000 drivers involved in fatal crashes have had their licenses suspended or revoked within the past 3 years. Moreover, "over 1,700 have had their licenses suspended or revoked three or more times, and about 100 whose licenses have been suspended or revoked ten or more times."[9] If I were ever paralyzed by a drunk driver with a record like that, I think I would be more enraged at the leniency of the State than the recklessness of the particular driver.

"There but for the grace of God go I" and all that, but America must wake up to the toll of allowing chronically alcoholic drivers, and other repeat offenders, back behind the wheel. Chances are, if you've been a dangerous driver, you'll remain a dangerous driver—and chances are, you'll drive anyway. The more years you do so, the more likely it is that you'll end up with a manslaughter charge.

Among the drunks and the reckless, the stoned, the visually impaired, and the uninsured, there is another class of suspended driver: the poor. And ironically, it is the poor—this last, *un*dangerous group—who can have the most difficulty getting their licenses back.

"In Wisconsin, you can lose your driver's license if you forget to pay your library fines, don't shovel the snow off your sidewalk, or don't trim a tree that overhangs a neighbor's property," reports Simson L. Garfinkel in his aptly titled *Wired* article, "Nobody Fucks with the DMV." He is no doubt referencing the DMV administrator Mrs. Hellberg in *License to Drive*: "You mustn't fuck with the Department of Motor Vehicles. We can make your life a living hell." In the America Garfinkel presents, "fucking with the DMV" is basically not being a good Boy Scout or Girl Scout in all realms of public life—or not having the financial means to make problems go away. In many states, the license has become, as Garfinkel points out, "a badge of good citizenship."

The license has become a behavioral modification tool, and taking it away is the ultimate punishment. This is part of the more general trend I have been describing: since the 1980s, the ID has completed its transition from a driving-related document to a document of extensive, even invasive, social control.

"Non-driving" suspensions vary, but usually are meant to incentivize the driver to repay debt. The first use of this was for enforcing child support payment in the 1980s. Its use has spread as states realize its astonishing efficacy. Threatening to suspend someone's license is the single most effective way to get Americans to pay up. Think about it: the no-license threat is even more effective than a court summons. And, unwilling to give up driving, virtually everyone who has the funds to pay their outstanding fines to avoid suspension does so.

That is, IF they receive their notification about the threatened suspended license. An even ever more common experience now is learning that your license is suspended— from the officer who just pulled you over for speeding. Aside from being a grade-A citizen, one can avoid this scenario by maintaining an up-to-date mailing address with the DMV.

But the people who *really* get in trouble are the people who can't pay. Unfortunately, these are precisely the people can't afford *not* to have a license: owning a car increases employment opportunity, and a suspended license greatly increases joblessness. "Driving is privilege, not right" is a point the state has inscribed on the minds of most Americans. But since when is basic mobility in a country notoriously short on public transportation a *privilege*?

"It's an economic death sentence," said one lawyer I interviewed, "for a lot of working-class folks."

"Spatial mismatch" is a term heard in America since the 1960s. It refers the fact that affordable housing is located in different areas than entry-level jobs—in other words, poor populations concentrated in inner cities don't have access to jobs in the suburban ring. Increasingly, however, it can refer to a mismatch between income ability and income demand: suburban workers with long commutes who struggle under the weight of both housing and transportation costs.

"A crime of poverty," is what David Powell, an Indiana prosecutor, called driving on a suspended license. "In my county, most of the cases I saw were people who couldn't afford their reinstatement fees so they just kept driving and just kept getting caught and caught and caught," he said.

It's such a common occurrence that it has a name: the "suspended license death spiral." The fees keep accumulating. Say you get your license revoked in Wisconsin for outstanding parking tickets you can't afford to pay. Then your side-view mirror gets sideswiped, and you can't afford to fix it. You get pulled over for the mirror, and are caught driving while suspended; the officer must automatically fine you $2,500. So now you have a whole list of things to pay for: the original parking tickets, the side-view mirror, the driving-while-suspended ticket, and when the time comes, the license reinstatement fee. Your job is across town from your apartment, and you can't afford to give up the job, and you can't imagine doing an hour minimum of public transportation to get there. So you drive, and everything is fine for a year or two. You're even saving up to pay the fees and get back on track. And then you get caught speeding, and now you're faced with another $5,000. The money you now owe represents about twenty-seven weeks of your minimum-wage job: half a year of work to pay the fees that started out as parking tickets. That's when the situation really starts to feel hopeless. Election season rolls around. You've always made a point of taking time off of work to vote. But since you've been forced to surrender your physical license (and didn't have the money, time, and energy to secure the necessary documents for a non-license photo ID), and since Wisconsin requires an ID for voting, you stay home from the polls.

Which gets me to the next issue.

Disenfranchisement

Thirty-six states have had, or have recently instituted, ID laws pertaining to voting. Two elections got the country talking about voting reform. The first, the popular election of Al Gore and the Supreme Court victory of George W. Bush, prompted a bipartisan commission on American voting. The co-chairs, Jimmy Carter and James A. Baker III, later summarized their proposal as "suggesting a uniform [e.g., nation-wide] voter photo ID … to be phased in over five years." The plan was that of widespread access in which, "States would provide free voter photo ID cards for eligible citizens; mobile units would be sent out to provide the IDs and register voters." But it was not to be—yet, at least. "No state has yet accepted our proposal," Carter and Baker wrote. "The laws on the books, mainly backed by Republicans, have not made it easy enough for voters to acquire an ID." The GOP took the voter-security idea and ran with it, using it for transparently obstructionist aims. Indiana was the first to get its law past the Supreme Court. That decision, back in 2008, opened the floodgates. As of 2014, Kansas, Texas, Arkansas, Mississippi, Tennessee, Georgia, and Virginia had laws just as strict on the books. Arizona, North Dakota, Louisiana, Alabama, Florida, and Rhode Island are not much more lenient. Indiana's law is now the national standard.

Then there are the states with less stringent ID requirements. In Alaska, you only need to present your ID if the election official doesn't know you personally. Missouri has a similar law; you have to be known by *two* election officials. In South Carolina and Alabama, you can vote without an ID, but only if you return to show officials your ID within a few days of the election. Montana, among other states, requests an ID, but if the voter does not have one, the election officials verify the voter's identity by comparing the signatures on the ballot and the voter registration. Idaho, Arizona, South Dakota, Wisconsin, Michigan, Kansas, Oklahoma, Texas, Arkansas, Louisiana, Mississippi, Tennessee, Florida, Georgia, South Carolina, North Carolina, Virginia, and Pennsylvania are among the states that have, or have had, voter ID laws.

To get a global sense of the significance of these headlines, I called Ari Berman, a staff reporter at *The Nation*, and one of our leading experts on voting rights.

"The legal trajectory is not a good one for voting rights right now," Berman said in our November 2013 conversation. "The legal side of it is really tough. Between the Supreme Court upholding Indiana [Crawford v. Marion County Election Board] and it striking down Section 4b [of the Voting Rights Act of 1965],[10] it's getting more difficult to challenge these types of laws." After Berman and I talked, progressives celebrated legal victories over voter ID laws in Wisconsin and Pennsylvania. But the Supreme Court precedent abides. And it threatens Americans' access to the most fundamental act of democracy.

A progressive position is not, *in theory*, opposed to requisite IDs to vote. The problem is that in practice, it amounts to widespread disenfranchisement—of women, the elderly, the poor, the dislocated—precisely those who aren't otherwise heard except at the ballot box. In Texas alone, between 600,000 and 800,000 registered voters do not have an ID to vote. The minimum cost for the documents to get one: $22 (Berman, Ari. "Will Texas Get Away With Discriminating Against Voters?" *The Nation*. September 1, 2014). If you're poor, $22 represents a week or more of food for the family. If you're poor, spending $22 for a piece of paper isn't an option. But here's the thing, y'all: poll taxes—that is, charging citizens to vote—have been illegal since the 24th Amendment to the US Constitution.

Even without the direct fees, though, opportunity costs and various other hurdles can obstruct voting access. (Keep in mind that everything is just more daunting when you're overworked and underslept, treated poorly at your minimum-wage job, and anxious about your kids.) Getting the ID entails tracking down a birth certificate, or maybe a social security card for a duplicate birth certificate, or a marriage certificate documenting a name change, or a car title, or current proof of insurance—and then perhaps spending a few hours on a bus to reach the nearest DMV (two counties away and not open on Saturdays). In Texas, there are DMVs in only eight-one of 254 counties. For a potential voter without a driver's license in a state without adequate public transportation, that fact alone can be a deal-breaker. Georgia, among other states, has recently tried to address this particular problem with mobile photo ID trucks, as per Jimmy Carter's urging.

"Dramatic voting restrictions in the past several years" reversed decades of increased access. Berman sees Lyndon Johnson's landmark Voting Rights Act of 1965 as launching an era of "expanding access to the ballot box," which continued until about 2008, when Obama's reelection galvanized a Republican effort to suppress Democratic turnout at the polls. Voter ID advocates claim the laws prevent voter impersonation. But—as Justices Souter and Ginsburg noted in their dissenting opinion in the Indiana case—voter impersonation is virtually unknown in the United States. In practice, voter ID laws are as tactical as gerrymandering.

University communities, almost invariably more politically progressive and geographically diverse than their environs, are hit particularly hard by the laws. In Texas, you can't vote with an out-of-state license, an expired license, or a student ID. You can, however, use a gun license. One young would-be Texas voter complained on Twitter during a recent election, "I can board a plane with my license, but I won't be able to vote today."[11]

Some Republican faithfuls explicitly admit the anti-Obama, anti-Democrat agenda. "I'm going to be real honest with you. The Republican Party doesn't want black people to vote if they are going to vote 9-to-1 for Democrats," said Tea Partier Ken Emanuelson at a 2013 rally in Texas.

A few months later, North Carolina GOP chair Don Yelton stunned viewers in a candid *Daily Show* interview about his state's voter ID laws. "The law is going to kick the Democrats in the butt. If it hurts a bunch of college kids that's too lazy to get off their bohunkus and get a photo ID, so be it. … If it hurts a bunch of lazy blacks that want the government to give 'em everything, so be it."[12] People who don't have IDs tend to be black, poor, urban, or out-of-state students. And they are overwhelmingly Democratic voters.

Most recently, we have Arizona Attorney General Tom Horne's first response to the ruling that his state could add special documentation requirements to voter registration over and above the federal requirements. He described the decision as "an important victory against the Obama administration." Not, you will note, an important victory against *voter fraud*. He spoke the truth.

Having lost in the Supreme Court, opponents of voter ID laws are having to work state by state, arguing in each court that the given voter ID law is a de facto poll tax disproportionately targeting society's most vulnerable groups. A more complicated question would involve a situation in which driver's licenses and other voter ID cards were free and easily accessible. Just how freely available would voter IDs have to be to be fair?

One problem with the free ID idea is that the states with voter ID laws tend to be the states with tax deficits. What if the state leadership decides under pressure to offer free voter IDs—but then doesn't provide the budget for them? Such was the case in Wisconsin back in 2011. Wisconsin Department of Transportation officials found a creative solution to the problem: they made non-license identity cards free on the books, but only gave them out as free if DMV patrons knew to demand that the $28 fee be waived. When an employee leaked the memo outlining this policy, DOT officials argued that the application form states the policy clearly in black and white anyway: the patron simply checks the box for "a product that is available for free issuance." (Free issuance? Come on, Badger State, just call it a "Free Identification Card.") Soon after, federal judges issued injunctions staying voter ID in Wisconsin. The star witness for the plaintiff? Professor Kenneth Mayer of the University of Wisconsin–Madison, who used census data to determine that about 220,000 constitutionally qualified Wisconsin voters lacked an ID that would allow them to vote. His research remains undisputed. Wisconsin now requires no ID.

Documenting
the undocumented

"Remove the document and you remove the man," says the Devil in Mikhail Bulgakov's Soviet fantasia, *The Master and Margarita*. In the United States, it doesn't quite work like that. Millions of undocumented Americans work, pay taxes and social security, raise children, go to college, own cars, pay auto insurance—and drive. Since late 2013, America has seen a wave of laws allowing people to get licenses regardless of citizenship status. The argument is that licensing all drivers allows states to make sure that all drivers understand the traffic laws and have insurance. California, home of about a quarter of the nation's undocumented residents, is scheduled to begin licensing its undocumented drivers in 2015.

As of March 2014, New Mexico, Washington, Illinois, Colorado, Utah, Nevada, Maryland, Connecticut, Vermont, Puerto Rico, and Washington, D.C., grant licenses regardless of immigration status. Oregon's law will go into effect pending a referendum. A dozen more state legislatures are debating similar laws.

On the other side of the spectrum, Arizona and Nebraska explicitly ban driver's licenses for so-called "Dreamers," young students who came to the United States illegally as children and have been granted "deferred action" from deportation. Arizona softened its laws in December 2013 to allow illegal immigrants to obtain licenses, if they were immediate family members of military personnel.

Meanwhile, an online vendor sells kids' T-shirts that read, "I can't get a license … and I *AM* a U.S. citizen!"

Again, this issue pits reality (undocumented Americans) against a competing ideal (no undocumented Americans). The states that license such drivers protect their residents against unsafe and uninsured drivers. The states that refuse to do so, refuse to accept reality. The realism/idealism fault line cuts through every social policy debate in America. The social reality (e.g., teens have sex) doesn't fit a competing ideal (teens don't have sex). If policy irrationally refuses to acknowledge reality (abstinence-only education for teens who have sex), the result is predictably disappointing (higher teen pregnancy rates among kids uneducated in preventive measures). Idealism may have been a value central to the founding of America, but that doesn't mean idealism won't prove our downfall. Or that pragmatism can't save us.

That's why the move toward licensing undocumented Americans, many of them the truest strivers and dreamers among us, is an encouraging sign.

Imagined futures

An Oregonian electrician recently told my mother this story. Long before his birth, his father came to the United States from Syria, and studied for several years to attain his US citizenship. Ten or so years later, a traffic policeman pulled him over for speeding and asked for his license. "It's posted," the father said. "I'm sorry, sir?" said the officer. "My license is posted right on the back of my car." "On the window?" the accommodating cop asked. "On the back of my car! I'm an American citizen. I have rights! You can't arrest me!" After more back and forth, the officer suddenly realized that the man thought a "license" was the license *plate*. Incredible as it may seem, after two decades in America, he had never known to get a driver's license. The officer let him off with a warning and directions to the DMV.

It's hard to fathom such confusion today; the license has risen to too great a prominence to slip by unknown, even by a newcomer in an alien culture. But viewed historically, the father's mistake is not so absurd. You may recall that driving-related licensing began not with the driver, but rather the car. And licensing may be returning, in part, to the car. In Nevada, in 2012, one year shy of the centennial of the first licenses issued to drivers in America, a Google-owned autonomous car received the first driverless driver's license.

Licenses—those plastic fetishes ornamented with regalia of security—signify a civic trust that their bearers will not endanger fellow citizens. Their social contract encompasses both law and ethics; computerized cars lack the latter. An autonomous car that follows driving laws to the letter may not, in fact, always be safer than a human capable of bending the rules for the greater good. As Cal Poly ethics professor Patrick Lin notes, "Human drivers can exercise judgment in a wide range of dynamic situations that don't appear in a standard 40-minute driving test; we presume they can act ethically and wisely."[13] Not that they always *do*, but that they *can*. The driverless car cannot. It cannot break the law, but neither can it draw from an ethical core when making split-second decisions about a puppy darting into the road, or the acutely ill child who needs to be rushed to the hospital on a near-empty parkway at three in the morning.

Technology and American identities: for over a century, the driver's license has mediated between them. At the dawn of the twentieth century, the automobile was America's "child of the century" and the public debated whether it was right to require a car owner to have a license to operate his or her own possession. Now at the start of the twenty-first, the car is an ill-conceived problem child, and the public raises eyebrows at the number of people under thirty-five who don't have driver's licenses. For many educated and urban young people, the license has more to do with a bar's ID scanner than with an automobile. The new function of license as *identity document* is superseding the original function of license as *driving document*. Over the next 100 years, as driving patterns will, necessarily, change in light of climate change, the driving part of the driver's license may become less important, even vestigial. The license's odd fusing of *driver* and *self* may become a quaint reminder of Americans long ago who went on joyrides and Sunday drives. We may see a rise in non–driver's license photo IDs as more young people opt not to drive. We may be spied upon by the government, or by hackers. We may eventually want crisp, clean, bright card designs. We may carry our health information within the RFID tags of our IDs, as they do in Germany and China. We may create mobile all-in-one ID trucks that help the poor and disenfranchised obtain identity documents like birth certificates, register for free photo IDs, and even sign up for public healthcare. We may decide that the children of today—largely unschooled in unstructured, face-to-face interactions—might actually benefit from a drinking culture not predicated on stealth. We might decide to give up the Reagan-era Prohibition and let them order champagne for their eighteenth birthdays. We may allow our roadways to crack, take seed, and devolve into open spaces for recreation and wildlife. We may truly commit to light rail and streetcars. We may slow down. We may develop identity cards that have nothing whatever to do with transportation—and we may even insist their design be gorgeous, crisp. We'll see—the future is open.

But for now, best keep the license on hand, *en garde*. It gets you through America.

NOTES

Chapter 1

1 Andy Warhol, *America* (New York: Penguin Popular Classics, 2011), 8.

Chapter 2

1 Thomas J. Knudson, "Drinking Age is Firey Issue in West," *The New York Times,* March 10, 1987.

2 "Year of First State Driver License Law and First Driver Examination," Federal Highway Administration, April 1997, accessed January 2014, https://www.fhwa.dot.gov/ohim/summary95/dl230.pdf

3 William DeJong and Jason Blanchette, "Case Closed: Research Evidence on the Positive Public Health Impact of the Age 21 Minimum Legal Drinking Age in the United States." *Journal of Studies on Alcohol and Drugs*, Supplement 75 (March 2014): 108–15.

4 John M. McCardell Jr, "What Your College President Didn't Tell You," *The New York Times*, September 13, 2004.

5 Amethyst Initiative, "Statement," accessed January 2014, http://www.theamethystinitiative.org/statement

6 For clarity and ease, I use the abbreviation DMV throughout this book. DMV is the most common name across the United States for the government agency responsible for issuing driver's licenses. There are, however, many differently named but equivalent bureaus—such as Massachusetts's RMV (Registry of Motor Vehicles) or Louisiana's OMV (Office of Motor Vehicles), Wyoming's WyDot (Department of Transportation) or Pennsylvania's PennDOT, and so on.

7 Jason Edward Harrington, "Dear America, I Saw You Naked," *Politico*, January 30, 2014.

8 Bruce Schneier, "Real-ID: Costs and Benefits," *The Bulletin of Atomic Scientists* 63 (March/April 2007): 55.

9 Bruce Schneier, "The TSA's Useless Photo ID Rules: No-fly lists and photo IDs are supposed to help protect the flying public from terrorists. Except that they don't work," *Los Angeles Times*, August 28, 2008, accessed February 2010, https://www.schneier.com/essay-236.html.

10 The group Privacy Activist, which works against Real-ID, puts the figure at over twenty billion dollars.

11 Kevin Poulsen, "The Secret Service Agent Who Collared Cybercrooks by Selling Them Fake IDs." *Wired* (July 22, 2013), accessed April 2, 2014, http://www.wired.com/2013/07/open-market/.

Chapter 3

1 Jesse McKinley, "Black and White and Wallet-Size, Unfit for Faking," *The New York Times*, March 16, 2013.

2 Frank Langfitt, "How I Flunked China's Driving Test. … Three Times," *NPR*, January 17, 2014, accessed February 1, 2014, http://www.npr.org/blogs/parallels/2014/01/17/263064557/how-i-flunked-chinas-driving-test-three-times

3 Langfitt, "How I Flunked China's Driving Test. … Three Times."

4 Langfitt, "How I Flunked China's Driving Test. … Three Times."

5 John Marzulli and Bill Hutchinson, "DMV guards, proxy test-takers arrested in New York driver's license scam," *New York Daily News*, September 25, 2013.

6 Langfitt, "How I Flunked China's Driving Test. … Three Times."

7 Lilia Sariecheva and Robert Osland, *My Russian Family*, Second edn, (Ventura, CA: Surepoint Publishing, 2009), 466.

8 "How is life for an American woman in Saudi Arabia?," accessed February 15, 2014, https://www.answers.yahoo.com/question/index?qid=20090719032917AAqKygM.

9 "Motor Bureau Stormed," *The New York Times*, June 29, 1922, accessed December 9, 2013, http://www.query.nytimes.com/mem/archive-free/pdf?res=F30A10F639551A738DDDA00A94DE405B828EF1D3.

10 Jearl Walker, Private Correspondence to Meredith Castile, November 11, 2013.

11 Jearl Walker, Private Correspondence to Meredith Castile.

12 "Driver's License Testing," accessed November 7, 2013, http://www.littledetails.livejournal.com/3051478.html

13 "We" here refers, of course, to non-indigenous Americans who have been in the country for generations, and who were not imported into the country as part of a program of absolute slavery or (as with the railroad-building Chinese) economic slavery.

14 *Blood and Oil*, directed by Jeremy Earp (Northhampton, MA: Media Education Foundation, 2008).

15 "Freedom," Dodge commercial, 2010, http://www.blog.chryslerllc.com/blog.do?id=1065&p=entry.

16 Betty Friedan, *The Feminine Mystique* (New York: W. W. Norton, 1963), 15.

Chapter 4

1 Tara Parker-Pope, "The Kids Are More Than All Right," *The New York Times*, February 2, 2012, accessed January 7, 2012, http://well.blogs.nytimes.com/2012/02/02/the-kids-are-more-than-all-right/?_php=true&_type=blogs&_r=0.

2 Alan Galsky and Joyce Shotick, "Managing Millennial Parents," *The Chronicle of Higher Education*, January 5, 2012, accessed February 2, 2012, http://www.chronicle.com/article/Managing-Millennial-Parents/130146.

3 Terry Castle, "Don't Pick Up: Why Kids Need to Separate from their Parents," *The Chronicle of Higher Education*, May 6, 2012, http://www.chronicle.com/article/The-Case-for-Breaking-Up-With/131760.

4 *License to Drive,* directed Greg Beeman (Century City: Twentieth Century Fox Film Corporation, 1988).

5 *License to Drive*, directed Greg Beeman.

6 "Home," accessed March 10, 2014, http://www.fearlessdriver.com.

7 N. B., "Commuting Makes You Unhappy," *The Economist*, June 4, 2011, http://www.economist.com/blogs/gulliver/2011/06/perils-commuting.

8 Elliot Chang, "America's Failing Infrastructure and the Need to Improve," *Inhabitat*, November 21, 2013, accessed January 5, 2014, http://www.inhabitat.com/infographic-americas-failing-infrastructure-and-the-need-to-improve.

9 Hope Yen, "Signs of Declining Economic Security," *Associated Press*, July 28, 2013.

10 Larissa Faw, "Why The Theory That Millennials Don't Care About Cars Is Wrong," *Forbes*, September 25, 2012, accessed January 4, 2012, http://www.forbes.com/sites/larissafaw/2012/09/25/why-the-theory-that-millennials-dont-care-about-cars-is-wrong.

Chapter 5

1 Sigmund Freud, "The Structure of the Unconscious," in *An Outline of Psychoanalysis*, trans. James Strachey (London, New York: W. W. Norton, 1949), 108.

2 Doon Arbus and Diane Arbus, *Diane Arbus: An Aperture Monograph* (New York: Aperture, 1972), 1.

3 Brigid Schulte, "Telling the Truth on License is Too Much for Some People," *The Washington Post*, October 8, 2008.

4 Brigid Schulte, "Telling the Truth on License is Too Much for Some People."

5 Mike Frassinelli, "Sixty-nine fake ID arrests made with help of 'facial recognition technology,'" *The Star-Ledger*, February 21, 2014.

6 ACLU, "ACLU Asks Florida Court to Reinstate Suspended Driver's License of Muslim Woman Forced to Remove

Her Face Veil," May 27, 2003, accessed November 8, 2013, https://www.aclu.org/religion-belief/aclu-asks-florida-court-reinstate-suspended-drivers-license-muslim-woman-forced-remo. ˙

7 Trenton Merricks, "There Are No Criteria of Identity Over Time." *Noûs* 32 (1998): 106.

8 An attorney now, Clarissa appended the following to her email: "Note that I was in Chicago most likely in violation of Illinois law because the state probably requires its residents to obtain an Illinois drivers' license after 90 days. Most states do that. While this doesn't mean the old license isn't valid, does mean that if Illinois ever caught me, I might have been required to have gotten a Illinois license." Theoretically, yes. But her doe-eyed, baby-faced fifteen-year-old picture is so shockingly adorable that I suspect the good cops of Chicago might turn a blind eye to her procedural violation.

9 Jacques Derrida, *Speech and Phenomena: And Other Essays on Husserl's Theory of Signs*, trans. David B. Allison (Evanston: Northwestern University Press, 1973), 129.

10 A quick note on terms: "Transgender" is an umbrella term for those who challenge the stark gender binary that organizes most of modern social life, from bathrooms to forms. Within the larger transgender category, the term "transsexual" describes a person who identifies with and transitions to the gender other than the one assigned at his or her birth.

11 Bob Egelko, "Transgender woman settles DMV suit," *San Francisco Chronicle*, August 15, 2011.

12 Victoria Michaels Lavelle, "Denied Gender Change at DMV: Government Workers Need More Education," *South Florida Gay News*, June 28, 2011, http://www.southfloridagaynews.

com/Columns/denied-gender-change-at-dmv-government-
workers-need-more-education.html.

13 Michel Foucault, *The Archaeology of Knowledge* (1969),
(New York: Knopf Doubleday Publishing Group, 2012), 17.

Chapter 6

1 Karl Koscher, "EPC RFID Tag Security Weaknesses and
Defenses: Passport Cards, Enhanced Drivers Licenses, and
Beyond," *Proceedings of the 16th ACM Conference on Computer
and Communications Security* (2009): 33–42.

2 Nicole Ozer, quoted in Dana Liebelson, "California Votes on
Driver's Licenses That Allow the Government (and Anyone
With $40) to Stalk You," *Mother Jones*, August 21, 2013,
http://www.motherjones.com/politics/2013/08/california-bill-
rfid-chip-personal-information.

3 RSA Laboratories, "A Primer on RFID," *RSA Industry
Perspectives*, accessed March 1, 2014, http://www.emc.com/
emc-plus/rsa-labs/research-areas/a-primer-on-rfid.htm.

4 RSA Laboratories, "A Primer on RFID."

5 Fidis, "Budapest Declaration on Machine Readable Travel
Documents," September 2006, http://www.fidis.net/press-
events/press-releases/budapest-declaration.

6 "Frequently asked questions: EDL/EID," Washington State
Department of Licensing, accessed March 3, 2014,
http://www.dol.wa.gov/driverslicense/edlfaq.html.

7 Unless, of course, you are black. In which case, the solution to
unwarranted police checks is decidedly less apparent.

8   *Unlicensed to Kill*, AAA Foundation for Traffic Safety, November 2011, accessed March 1, 2014, https://www.aaafoundation.org/sites/default/files/2011Unlicensed2Kill.pdf.

9   *Unlicensed to Kill*, AAA Foundation for Traffic Safety.

10 Section 4 of the Voting Rights Act of 1965 contained the formula for how to determine whether a jurisdiction had a history of voter discrimination. It was struck down in 2013's *Shelby County v. Holder*. Section 5 of the Act, also struck down, authorized federal oversight of jurisdictions with histories of discrimination.

11 Dana Liebelson, "Voter ID Laws in Action: 'Looks Like I Don't Get to Vote Today,'" *Mother Jones*, 6 November 2013, http://www.motherjones.com/politics/2013/11/voter-supression-id-election-day-virginia-texas.

12 Aasif Mandvi, "Interview with Don Yelton," *The Daily Show with Jon Stewart*, Comedy Central, October 23, 2013, http://thedailyshow.cc.com/videos/dxhtvk/suppressing-the-vote?mode=jqm.

13 Patrick Lin, "The Ethics of Autonomous Cars," *The Atlantic*, October 8, 2013, accessed March 15, 2014, http://www.theatlantic.com/technology/archive/2013/10/the-ethics-of-autonomous-cars/280360.

ACKNOWLEDGMENTS

Without whom, nothing: John Walker, Carol Castile, Franco Moretti, Liz Moloney, Dardis McNamee, Catherine Wilhelm, Zoë Jay, and most immediately and directly, Carston Johannsen. With loving thanks to the wide net of family, friends, and new contacts who contributed anecdotes, ideas, image, and interviews. *Vielen herzlichen Dank* for the faith and vision of Christopher Schaberg, Haaris Naqvi, Ian Bogost, and Bloomsbury.

For C., for the visa. And for S., for the *ja*.

INDEX

ACLU *see* American Civil
    Liberties Union (ACLU)
Acoff, Cemia Dove   107
Adams, Mike   38, 39
Alabama   122
Alaska   32, 108, 122
Alm, Niko   99–101
America
    activism   23
    car culture   60, 61–6, 74–5,
        77, 78, 131–2
    crime   5, 32, 33, 34,
        38–40, 73, 96
    discrimination   105–11
    drinking   4–5, 6, 11, 14,
        21–2, 24–6, 131
    driving regulations   54–60
    exceptionalism   61–2,
        99, 100
    expansionism   61, 62
    idealism   60, 113, 129
    identity   3, 130–2
    immigration   113, 127–9

individualism   4, 5, 62,
    96–101
interstate system   65, 77
legislation   3, 4–5, 10,
    30, 113
licensing
    regulations   54–60
mythos   3–4
national security   6, 9–10,
    25–30, 33, 37–8, 46, 55,
    116, 130
personal freedom   3, 5, 11
politics   5–6, 23, 121–8
poverty   80–1, 118–21,
    125–6
privacy   2, 108, 113–17
public transportation   3,
    62, 65, 120, 121, 124
religious freedom   96–101
social control   5, 113–32
states' rights   7–9, 10,
    54–60, 121–9
surveillance   9, 113–17

teen culture   67–82, 129, 132
terrorism   6, 9, 10, 26, 30, 33, 49
voting   23–4, 113, 121
American Association of Motor Vehicle Administrators   31
American Civil Liberties Union (ACLU)   97–8
Amethyst Initiative   22–3, 24
Apple   15, 79, 82
Arbus, Diane   89–90
Arizona   102, 122, 123, 126, 128
Arkansas   53, 122, 123
Atari   70
Atlantic   17
Austria   49, 51, 99–101
Autobahn   64

Back to the Future (Zemeckis)   70
Baker, James A. III   122
Beeman, Greg   74
   License to Drive   67, 68, 73–6, 79–80, 118–19
Belgium   10
Beloit College   68–9
Berman, Ari   123–5
biometrics   95–6
Blade Runner (Scott)   70
Boggan, Steven   115

Bonnie and Clyde   58
Boys and Girls Clubs   34
Boys Don't Cry (Peirce)   106–7
Breakfast Club   74
Buchholz, Todd   78
Buchholz, Victoria   78
Bulgakov, Mikhail   127
   The Master and Margarita   127
Burr, Ginger   93
Bush, George W.   5, 6, 30, 122
   War on Terror   6

California   28, 59–60, 77, 78, 104, 108, 110–11, 127
California Department of Transportation   65
California Polytechnic State University (Cal Poly)   130
Cal Poly *see* California Polytechnic State University (Cal Poly)
Cameron, James
   The Terminator   70
Canada   53, 117
Canadian Bank Note Technologies (CBN)   45
car culture   61–6, 74–5, 78, 131–2
   Americanness   62
   branding   62–4
   commuting   77

consumerism   63–4
economics   63, 65–6
feminism   64
Fordism   63
freedom   62, 63, 64
interstate system   65, 77
marketing   62–4
public transportation   65
suburbia   63–4
tradition   62–3
Carroll, Lewis   102, 103
Carter, Jimmy   122, 124
Castillo, Eddie   98
Castle, Terry   72
CBN *see* Canadian Bank Note
    Technologies (CBN)
China   37, 45, 49–50,
    51, 131
civil disobedience   23
Cleveland   107
Clueless (Heckerling)   70
Coalition for a Secure Driver's
    License (CSDL)   33–6
Cold War   64–5
Colorado   7, 97, 128
Connecticut   128
counterfeits *see* fakes
*Crawford v. Marion County
    Election Board*   123
crime *see* fakes; identity theft
CSDL *see* Coalition for
    a Secure Driver's License
    (CSDL)

*Daily Show with Jon
    Stewart*   125
Dean, James   67, 68
Dear America, I Saw You
    Naked (Harrington)   27
Democrats   125, 126
Denmark   27
Department of Homeland
    Security   26, 31, 32, 114
    see also Transportation
    Security Administration
    (TSA)
Department of Motor
    Vehicles (DMV)   12,
    26, 29, 32, 34, 43, 45,
    57–8, 65, 89, 90, 91,
    92, 93, 94, 95, 104, 105,
    108–9, 116, 118–19, 124,
    126, 129
    no-smiling rules   95–6
Derrida, Jacques   103
DiMaggio, Joe   60
disenfranchisement   121–8
DMV *see* Department of Motor
    Vehicles (DMV)
Document Security Alliance
    (DSA)   33, 47
Doogie Howser, M.D.   70
drinking   21–2, 51–2, 53, 54,
    55, 89, 118
    abstinence   22, 24
    bingeing   5, 21–2
    laws   4–5, 6, 7

legislation   7–9, 21, 22, 23, 24
moderation   24
National Minimum Drinking Age Act of 1984   7–9
Prohibition   5
underage   5, 6, 7–9, 11–14, 21–2, 24–6, 32, 34–5, 36, 59, 132
Drive My Car (McCartney-Lennon)   74
Driver's License Redesign (Jencks)   41–5
drugs   6, 14
War on Drugs   6
DSA *see* Document Security Alliance (DSA)
Dust Bowl   58

Economist   77
EDL *see* Enhanced Driver's License (EDL)
EID *see* Enhanced ID (EID)
Eisenhower, Dwight D.   64
Emmanuelson, Ken   125
Enhanced Driver's License (EDL)   117
Enhanced ID (EID)   117
Europe   45, 51, 54, 115
   see also individual countries
European Union   115
E-ZPass   116

Facebook   70
facial recognition software   95–6
fakes   7–10, 11–21, 23, 24, 28–9, 32–3, 34–40, 45, 59, 84, 85–7, 102, 107
China   37, 45
costs   18
crime   35–6, 38–40, 45, 85
digitization   16, 83
economics   37–8
holograms   16
identity theft   19–20, 32, 34, 37
Internet   37–40
lamination   11, 12, 14, 15
legal risks   17, 19, 25
materials   15, 16, 20, 37
outsourcing   37–40
painting   83–8
photography   83–101, 105
properties   37
psychology   19–20
quality   20, 32–3, 37
Russia   38, 39–40, 45
Säker, Fredrik Danger   83–8
seizures   19–20
sexual violence   35–6
technology   37
templates   115
terrorism   25–6, 29, 30, 33
torrent sites   15, 16

traceability   16
underage drinking   11–14, 35, 36
viability   17–18, 32–3
Falsetti, Tony   90
Fantelli, Rachel   109
Faw, Larissa   82
Feldman, Corey   74
Feminine Mystique, The (Friedan)   64
Fidis *see* Future of Identity in the Information Society (Fidis)
Fight Club (Fincher)   28
Fincher, David
    Fight Club   28
Florida   17, 97, 98, 108–9, 122, 123
Florida Department of Highway Safety and Motor Vehicles   97
Forbes   92
Fordism   63, 76
Ford Motor Company   63, 76
    Fordism   63, 76
forgeries *see* fakes
Foucault, Michel   111
France   53, 54
Freeman, Sultana LaKiana Myke   97–8
Freud, Sigmund   89
Friedan, Betty   64
    The Feminine Mystique   64

Future of Identity in the Information Society (Fidis)   115

Gansler, Doug   36
Garfinkel, Simson L.   118–19
    Nobody Fucks with the DMV   118–19
gender discrimination   105–11
General Motors (GM)   62
Georgia   122, 123, 124
Germany   51, 53, 131
GM *see* General Motors (GM)
Google   130
GOP *see* Republicans
Gore, Albert (Al)   122
Graham, Heather   74
Great Britain   53, 115
Guardian   115

Haim, Corey   74
Harrington, Jason Edward   26–9
    Dear America, I Saw You Naked   27
Harvard University   29, 82
Heckerling, Amy
    Clueless   70
Hiroshima   10
Hitler, Adolph   64
Horne, Tom   126
Hughes, John
    Sixteen Candles   70

Hulu   70
Hurley, Peter   93–5

Idaho   7, 123
idem et idem   103
identification
    accessibility   26
    aesthetics   45
    archiving   31
    authentication   83
    costs   80
    database   31–2
    Department of Motor
        Vehicles   12, 26, 29,
        32, 34, 43, 45, 57–8, 65,
        89, 90, 91, 92, 93, 94,
        95, 104, 105, 108–9,
        116, 118–19, 124, 126,
        127, 130
    design   33, 41–5, 47, 48,
        56, 99, 116
    digitization   12, 30, 32, 83
    discrimination   105–11
    disenfranchisement   121–7
    document screening   26–36
    dreaming   60
    drinking   11, 14, 21–2, 23,
        24–6, 34–5, 51–2, 53, 54,
        55, 59, 89, 118, 131
    driving   10, 31, 50–1,
        56–60, 74, 131
    economics   55–6, 60, 80–1,
        116, 119, 120, 121–8

ego   88–91, 92–3
eligibility   51–4
fakes   7–10, 11–21, 23, 24,
    28–9, 32–3, 34–40, 45,
    59, 84, 85–7, 102, 107
fluorescence   28
forensics   90
freedom   2, 96–101
functionality   42
gender   105–11
global market   10
headshots   93–5
history   9–10, 54–60
identity theft   19–20, 32,
    38–40, 115
immigration   113, 127–9
inconsistencies   105–11
informality   59–60
integrity   33
intimacy   2
invincibility   47–8
lamination   9, 11, 12, 14,
    15, 17, 48, 58
law enforcement   31–2, 33
legislation   2, 10, 24,
    30–2, 33, 54–5, 56,
    95–6, 121–9
as leverage   9
memento mori   87
nationalization   2
new technology   30, 31,
    33, 45, 95–6, 113–17,
    130–2

no-smiling rules   95–6
objectification   2
obsolescence   102–6
officialdom   2
orientation   43, 48
passports   17, 27–8, 49, 52, 85, 105, 114, 115, 116–17
permission   1
personal identity   101–11, 131–2
photgeneity   94
photographic   8–9, 15, 29–30, 31–2, 38, 42, 43–4, 45, 53, 83–101
physical markers   110–11
policing   9
politics   98–101, 121–8
poverty   80–1, 118–21, 125–6
privacy   2, 108, 113–17
properties   28, 45, 46, 56
Radio Frequency Identification (RFID)   113–17, 131
religion   96–101
repression   36
security   2, 6, 9–10, 11, 17, 25, 26–36, 37, 43, 44, 46–7, 55, 115, 130
seizures   19–20
self-deception   88–91

semiotics   28
social control   9, 88–9, 97–8, 105–11, 113–32
standardization   2, 30, 31, 41, 42, 48, 59
surveillance   113–17
suspension   113, 117–21
talisman   1
testing   10, 31, 50–1, 56–60, 74, 131
traceability   16
validation   2, 29, 42, 83–7
viability   17–18
voting   23–4, 113, 121–7
youth   5–6, 9, 11–12, 14–15, 21–2, 23–4, 25, 34–5, 59, 67–82, 128–9, 131
identity theft   19–20, 32, 33, 34, 37, 39, 115
Illinois   97, 128
Impossibility of Religious Freedom, The (Sullivan)   97
Indiana   97, 120, 122, 123
Instagram   70
Intelligence Reform and Terrorism Prevention Act of 2004   30
Internet   37–40, 69–70
iPhone   70
Iran   52

Jackson, Michael   70
James, Henry   78
Japan   27–8, 52–3
Jencks, Robert   41–5
   Driver's License
     Redesign   41–5
Johnson, Lyndon   124

Kansas   53, 98, 122, 123
Kansas City   12–14
Kentucky   32
Kerouac, Jack   61
   On the Road   61
Kirby, Jennifer   80–1
Kyle, Margaret Beatrice
   110–11

LaFrance, Adrienne   17
Lamb, Thomas   39
Langfitt, Frank   50, 51
Latvia   53
Lavelle, Victoria
   Michaels   108–9
Legal Consequences of
   Underage Drinking and
   Sexual Assault   35–6
Lennon, John
   Drive My Car   74
License to Drive (Beeman)   67,
   68, 73–6, 79–80, 118–19
Lin, Patrick   130
Los Angeles Times   29–30
Louisiana   55, 122, 123

Lucas, George
   Star Wars   70
Luxembourg   63

McCardell, John   22
McCarthyism   5
McCartney, Paul
   Drive My Car   74
Madonna   70
Magritte, René   87–8
   *The Treachery of
     Images*   87–8
Maine   32
Manifest Destiny   61
Marshall, Randall   98
Maryland   36, 55, 109–10, 128
Massachusetts   32
Master and Margarita, The
   (Bulgakov)   127
Mayer, Kenneth   127
Merricks, Trenton   101–2
Michigan   123
Middlebury College   22
Miller, Cheryl   47
Milwaukee   107
Mississippi   53, 55, 122, 123
Missouri   122
Monaco   63
Montana   7, 28, 55, 123
Mottett, Lisa   106, 108–10

Nagasaki   10
Napster   70

Nation 123
National Center for Transgender
  Equality 106
National Conference of State
  Legislators 31
National Governors
  Association 31
National Minimum Drinking
  Age Act of 1984 7–9,
  22, 24, 32
National Public Radio
  (NPR) 50
National Security Agency
  (NSA) 32, 114
Nebraska 97, 107, 128
Netherlands, the 53, 115
Nettles, Islan 107
Nevada 38–9, 128, 130
New Jersey 17, 30, 45, 96,
  98–9, 100
New Jersey Motor Vehicle
  Commission 96, 98–9
New Mexico 128
New York 9, 44–5, 50–1,
  56–8
New York City 25, 41,
  58, 107
New York Times 7, 22,
  58, 78
9/11 *see* September 11, 2001
9/11 Commission Report 25–6
Nobody Fucks with the DMV
  (Garfinkel) 118–19

No-Fly List 29
North Carolina 91, 123, 125
North Dakota 122
Norway 53
no-smiling rules 95–6
NPR *see* National Public Radio
  (NPR)
NSA *see* National Security
  Agency (NSA)

Oakland (CA) 110–11
Obama, Barack 125, 126
Ohio 7
Oklahoma 123
On the Road (Kerouac) 61
Oregon 55, 128
Osland, Robert 51

passports 17, 27–8, 49,
  52, 85, 105, 114, 115,
  116–17
  see also identification
Pastafarians 98, 99
Peirce, Kimberly
  Boys Don't Cry 106–7
Pennsylvania 56, 123
personal identity 101–11,
  131–2
Pfizer 114
Philadelphia 107
Photoshop 14
Pinterest 70
Pitt, Brad 28

political activism   23
Politico   27
Poulsen, Kevin   38
Powell, David   120
Presley, Elvis   10
Prohibition   5, 59
Puerto Rico   128

Radio Frequency Identification
    (RFID)   113–17, 131
Ray, Nicholas
    *Rebel Without a
    Cause*   67–8
Reagan, Ronald   5–6, 9, 21,
    22, 32, 131
    War on Drugs   6
REAL ID Act   30–1, 32, 36, 116
Real ID Act: National Impact
    Analysis (2007)   31
Rebel Without a Cause
    (Ray)   67–8
religious freedom   96–101
Republicans   5–6, 30, 122, 125
RFID *see* Radio Frequency
    Identification (RFID)
Rhode Island   122
Russia   38, 39–40, 45, 51–2

Säker, Fredrik Danger   83–8
San Diego Union-Tribune   109
Saudi Arabia   52
Schaberg, Christopher   28
Schneier, Bruce   29–30

Schoettle, Brandon   71
Scott, Ridley
    Blade Runner   70
Secret Service   38–40
Sensenbrenner, James
    (Jim)   30
September 11, 2001   14, 25,
    29, 47, 97
Ship of Theseus   101–2
Sivak, Michael   71
Sixteen Candles (Hughes)   70
Skype   69, 70
Smithsonian   47
Societal Costs of Fake
    IDs   34–6
Sontag, Susan   84
South Carolina   122, 123
South Dakota   7, 10, 123
squinching   94–5
Stanford University   72
Star Wars (Lucas)   70
Sullivan, Winnifred Fallers   97
    *The Impossibility of Religious
    Freedom*   97
Supreme Court *see*
    U.S. Supreme Court
suspended license death
    spiral   120–1
Sweden   53, 83–7
Switzerland   51

Tate, Hardy   7
Tea Party   125

teen culture 67–82, 128–9, 131
  adulthood 71–3
  cars 67–8
  connectivity 69–70
  consumerism 68
  counterculture 68
  driving 67–8, 70–80, 81–2
  freedom 67, 68, 76
  neo-futurism 70
  poverty 80–1
  public transportation 82
  rebellion 67–8
  social media 37–40, 69, 70, 78, 130
  social status 70, 80, 82
  technology 68, 69, 70, 71–3
  underage drinking 5, 6, 7–9, 11–14, 21–2, 24–6, 32, 34–5, 36, 59, 131
Tennessee 9, 122, 123
Terminator, The (Cameron) 70
Texas 11, 58–9, 96, 122, 123–4, 125
Texas Tech 98
Thoreau, Henry David 23
Trafikverket 84
Transportation Research Institute 71
Transportation Security Administration (TSA) 2, 26–30, 37, 46, 96

Travolta, John 67
Treachery of Images, The (Magritte) 87–8
TSA *see* Transportation Security Administration (TSA)
Twitter 70, 78

Ultimate Fake ID Guide V8 16
underage drinking *see* drinking; teen culture
University of Michigan 71
University of Wisconsin–Madison 127
USA PATRIOT Act 30
U.S. Constitution 24, 124
U.S. Department of Defense 114
U.S. Supreme Court 7, 122, 123, 126
Utah 128

Vermont 55, 128
Vietnam War 23
Virginia 28, 45, 122, 123
voting 23–4, 113, 121–7
  see also disenfranchisement; Voting Rights Act of 1965
Voting Rights Act of 1965 123, 124–5

Wall of Shame   19, 20
Wal-Mart   114
Warhol, Andy   3
War on Drugs   6
War on Terror   6
Washington   116–17, 128
Washington, DC   25, 33,
      106, 128
Western Hemisphere
      Travel Initiative
      (WHTI)   116–17
Westhues, Jonathan   115
Wharton, Edith   78
WHO *see* World Health
      Organization (WHO)
WHTI *see* Western Hemisphere
      Travel Initiative (WHTI)

Willey, P.   90
Williams, Aaron   99, 100
Williams, Diamond   107
Wired   38, 118–19
Wisconsin   118, 120–1, 123,
      126–7
World Health Organization
      (WHO)   51
Wyoming   7, 10, 53

Yelton, Don   125
Young, Evon   107
youth culture *see* teen culture
YouTube   70

Zemeckis, Robert
      Back to the Future   70